EX LIBRIS

VINTAGE **CLASSICS**

TOM PAYNE

Tom Payne was born in 1971. He read Classics at Corpus Christi College, Cambridge and was deputy literary editor of the *Daily Telegraph*. He now lives with his wife and four children in Dorset, where he teaches English and Classics at Sherborne School and Latin at the Gryphon School. His previous books are *Fame: From the Bronze Age to Britney* and a verse translation of Ovid's *The Art of Love*.

TOM PAYNE

The Ancient Art of Growing Old

VINTAGE

1 3 5 7 9 10 8 6 4 2

Vintage
20 Vauxhall Bridge Road,
London SW1V 2SA

Vintage Classics is part of the Penguin Random House
group of companies whose addresses can be found at
global.penguinrandomhouse.com

Copyright © Tom Payne 2015

Tom Payne has asserted his right to be identified
as the author of this Work in accordance with the Copyright,
Designs and Patents Act 1988

First published in Great Britain by Vintage Classics in 2015

www.vintage-books.co.uk

A CIP catalogue record for this book is available
from the British Library

ISBN 9780099573180

Printed and bound by Clays Ltd, St Ives plc

Penguin Random House is committed to a sustainable future
for our business, our readers and our planet. This book is made
from Forest Stewardship Council® certified paper.

To Louise
(You make me unafraid of age)

Contents

Preface

If I'd known I would have lived this long, I'd have taken better care of myself.

Eubie Blake, American jazz musician (1887–1983)[1]

This is a book for young people as well as for those experiencing old age. As the ancients knew, young people don't want to think about growing old. But they should, because the prospects of reaching old age are increasingly likely, and if there's one thing about old age on which the ancients could agree, it's this: that you must prepare for it. A good old age is the reward of a good life, and the memory of your achievements and faith in your virtue will make all the more bearable any privations or problems that old age has in store for you. Professor Robert Garland puts the problem elegantly: 'True wisdom was perceived to be a function of old age and conversely that old age can be attained by living wisely.'[2]

Yes, to a young person, this can sound like so much rhetoric, and Roman rhetoric at that. An orator dispensing this kind of wisdom will come across as someone who wishes that youths would behave and show more respect to their elders; the insistence on virtue seems to be a way of keeping the kids in check.

The ancients go further. The extremely old Gorgias claimed that the reason he reached so great an age was because he never accepted dinner invitations. So, avoid excessive pleasure. Train the body. Train the mind. Keep the mind active. Retain an interest in public affairs. None of this feels at all fashionable, and not just because much of it comes from an era before Christ; it also chimes with the kind of muscular Christianity that you might hear from a schoolmaster.

I must have thought so once. Then I became a parent, and then a schoolteacher. Getting to know more about children has made me think even more about the elderly. It's fitting that when Cicero writes about old age, he uses the voice of Cato, an old man from generations earlier, and has him address two young men, one of whom hopes that 'we could learn from you long in advance the thinking by which we might bear the growing weight of old age more easily'. Cicero imagines splendid young men from that bygone era (as if adding under his breath, 'Those were the days') who not only respected their elders but also were excited about becoming older.

Perhaps this was a hard sell, even in Cicero's time. But there are gentler ways of putting it. Some even suggest that we can be fairly mature before we start worrying too much: the geriatrician Olivier de Ladoucette explains, 'Of course, ageing well demands that you have a healthy life, stay physically active, eat well, and have social life. And you can't improvise all this at the age of 75. You must be thinking about it from the age of sixty.'[3] This is a reassuringly relaxed perspective. But shouldn't we be a little more vigilant a lot sooner? After all, our younger years are the time when we come to know ourselves. We explore our limits. If we go too far, we may learn not to go so far the next time. And youth is the time to learn. Seneca says that it is good to study at any age, but not always to learn: an old man learning his ABC would be an embarrassment. If we gather knowledge when we're young, we can use it when we're old. Plato is keen that we sustain our use of it too. As Socrates explains, 'It's right to go on learning as long as you live, and are prepared to do so because you don't assume that wisdom is an automatic consequence of old age.'[4]

Galen, the ancient physician, had enough illnesses to have worked out what remedies worked for him; and for commentators on old age knowing what does and doesn't help you is a great advantage. You could argue from this that *not* having a virtuous life and making enough mistakes from which to learn is another sort of preparation for old age. But, however good the doctors of the ancient Mediterranean were, they weren't so good that they could reverse the injuries a young person could inflict on the body in which he or she might be stuck for a long while.

Still, if this book is to be any use for the young or the

old, it will be because whatever advice it offers can be taken or rejected depending on the temperament or needs of the reader. The old men and women we will meet lived in a distant time, and lots of what they experienced won't be our experience. Some of it might; but even when we encounter the differences, we come to know ourselves a little better.

There is another reason why this is a book for the young. Even if we're not interested in old age when we're young, we should at least concern ourselves with the elderly. There may well be aspects of growing old in antiquity that alarm us, but the ancients would be alarmed by aspects of our own society too. The debates today about the attitudes of a younger generation towards an older one make it clear that we're at least concerned about it. I don't want to trivialise those debates by saying that among the most moving and helpful contributions to them is *Gangsta Granny* by David Walliams. It makes the point that children can enjoy learning about the exploits of their grandparents, just as the grandparents can enjoy the memory of those exploits (even if they were mostly in the sphere of international jewel theft). Crucially, it makes the point directly to children.

If you pick up a previous book about old age in antiquity, you're likely to be told that there haven't been many serious studies of the subject. That has been true. But recently some authors have produced ground-breaking work in this area – Robert Garland, Karen Cokayne and the particularly impressive Tim Parkin, whose *Old Age in the Roman World* manages to be both thorough and thought-provoking.[5] These writers are great authorities on the ancient world, but they also respond to the increasing difficulty we have in answering questions about our own community of elderly people, which continues to grow. My fervent hope is that their work is as useful to undergraduates (and still younger students) as it is to more senior researchers.

What follows draws heavily on their work, even if I am sometimes taken to different conclusions. There are sufficient gaps in our knowledge, even now, to invite a range of interpretations, and even speculations, which are inevitably guided by our own perspectives and experiences. My offering is an attempt to test some of the literature about the elderly, and some of their history, against our own positions.

It is also an attempt to give some context to the second part of the book, Cicero's dialogue called *Cato Maior de Senectute – Cato the Elder on Old Age*, which I present, after a flurry of letter-writing from Seneca the Younger. This is a text that has become less venerated the less scholars have thought antiquity to be a golden age for old people, and the setting of Cicero's dialogue is already nostalgic enough.[6] If read as social history, it does absolutely present us with an idealised old man espousing a good life so blessed that even he has to admit he's particularly lucky. But it can also be read as literature or philosophy, and in those genres idealism is not only forgivable but maybe even desirable. After all, we're not only discussing the realities of being old, but how writers and thinkers expressed their feelings about the elderly and about ageing.

It would be trite to offer a third reason why this is a book for the young by saying that it's for the young at heart. So I won't, because it isn't. Cicero might have made his Cato say, 'That's why I approve of the young person who has something of the elderly about him, and the old person in whom there's a bit of youth – because someone observing this may be old in body, but never in mind.' And where I work there is a bust of Frederick Temple, schoolmaster and bishop, below which are two Latin elegiac couplets that praise him for being for ever a boy, even when an old man. But really the ancients are at their most persuasive – and invite the most empathy – when they are contemplating the joys that are particular to old age. If parts of our psyches can remain youthful, even into maturity, then hurray; but it seems risky to expect this, and surer (as Seneca suggests) to act as though new benefits await: 'The most blessed, and most secure people are the self-possessed ones who wait for tomorrow without anxiety. Whoever has said, "I lived" rises to a reward every day.'

Cast List

The following characters will appear frequently in our discussion of old age, and it is worth giving them a brief introduction.

Aristophanes (Athenian comic playwright, c.455–386 BC) – Aristophanes makes jokes about everyone, so the jokes about the elderly in Aristophanes' plays don't necessarily suggest that he disliked them. In *Clouds*, a young man ends up hitting his father over the head, and using the debating techniques he picked up from Socrates to justify himself. Although Socrates is the butt of the joke, there would have been laughter, too, in the shock (or familiarity?) of a youngster disrespecting his elders. In *The Women of the Assembly*, old women use their newfound powers to demand sex with young men: here the joke goes on long enough to suggest a lurid fascination with the idea that older women can have desires. Aristophanes' most political portrayal of the elderly is in *Wasps*, in which the playwright mocks people power by showing that juries in big court cases end up being old, poorish men with nothing better to do. Throughout these comedies, Aristophanes plays on the stereotypes of the elderly, sometimes by taking the caricature further, and sometimes by flipping his audience's expectations.

Aristotle (384–322 BC) – However great a philosopher Aristotle was, he is an uncomforting voice on old age. As a scientist, he explained how ageing is a process of drying, and how the organs lose their vital moisture. As a teacher of rhetoric, he went further in making old age seem awful: speakers need to know that the elderly think about the past, and themselves, and are stingy. As you'll see, he goes further.

Cato the Elder (Roman statesman, 234–149 BC) – Cicero articulates his theories about old age through the historical figure of Cato the Elder. Cato fought against Hannibal under Scipio Africanus, and rose through the track of honours. He opposed Greek customs; voted against repealing a law that forbade women from wearing flamboyant jewellery in times of national emergency; repeatedly demanded that Carthage be destroyed; rooted out corruption wherever he found it; and took as his last office the role of censor.

For these reasons, he becomes for Cicero a model of Rome's glorious past, and shows the practical advantages of a modest, restrained lifestyle. Cato was also a historian, and an agriculturalist who wrote extensively in praise of cabbages, and so (to Cicero at least) personified the virtues of old age: a veneration of the past, and a love of the continuity nature can bring, especially in the form of plants. See also the introduction to *On Old Age*.

Cicero (106–43 BC) – Roman statesman, orator and philosopher; see introduction to *On Old Age*.

Epicurus (341–270 BC) – a philosopher, born in Samos. The Epicurean school of philosophers, based in Athens, was named after him. Although his name is associated with indulgence and hedonism, his notions of pleasure were more illuminating than to say, 'Have a good time all the time.' According to the later writers who explained his thinking (especially the Latin poet Lucretius), his views were more moral: living a good life takes consideration and moderation, since life is as much about avoiding discomfort as it is about seeking comfort, and an excess of pleasure can lead to discomfort. Cicero, who sees himself as a Stoic thinker in *On Old Age*, and therefore opposed to what many considered 'Epicurean' philosophy, in fact ends up sounding a lot like the Epicurus who would argue for restraint as a way of ensuring long-term happiness, especially when Cicero is discussing the damage a licentious youth can do to one's dotage. However, Cicero parts company with Epicurus more noticeably when discussing death and the afterlife: Epicureans did not believe in the soul.

Galen (Greek physician, born in Pergamon, 129 AD; dates for his death range from 199–216 AD) – Galen conducted a huge amount of medical research, sometimes by experiments on animals (including monkeys) and often by observing his patients, including himself. His conclusions about old age differed from those of earlier commentators, who thought of ageing as a disease (Seneca was among these). For Galen, old age was natural and inevitable. He emphasised the idea that each individual experience of old age is different, and the speed with which it arrives is down to our humours, or the balance of hot, cold, wet and dry elements in our bodies. For him, as for Aristotle, ageing was at once a cooling process and a drying process. How to deal with it is again a matter for the individual. In keeping with modern physicians, he prioritised prevention rather than cure: eating the right foods, and taking regular, but not hazardous, exercise (this would allay the cooling process). Baths could delay the inevitable drying that old age was thought to bring. Like Seneca, he recommended conversation; undiluted wine was not a bad idea; the game of snatching a ball (called Harpastum); and being carried about in a litter.

Hesiod (Greek poet, eighth century BC) – In his poem, *Works and Days*, Hesiod describes the five ages of man, from the golden age down to the age of iron. As the eras go on, humans age more, and sooner, and the young become apt to pick fights with their elders.

Homer (Greek poet; the Homeric poems appeared in written form in the eighth century BC) – Homer's depictions of his old characters imbue them with dignity. In the *Iliad*, Nestor is highly valued as a counsellor – at least, until we start reading between the lines. His advice can be wrong, and he spends a long time talking, often to say how good a talker he is. Even in the eighth century, Greeks were writing epigrams about what a windbag he was. Homer's more developed and intriguing representations of old age come in the *Odyssey*, in which the hero is the model of a man who prevails through experience and wily tactics as much as through action, and in doing so presents the idea advanced by Solon, Cicero, Plutarch, and for that matter, Nestor: that the prime of life is for warriors, and the next phase is for steering the state, and offering the benefit of wisdom taken from the past.

Horace (65–8 BC) – Roman poet, who often adopted the persona of an older man looking back fondly on his past, enjoying the pleasures of wine and flirtation, and treating the attractions of public life with genial indifference. His best-known poem (*Odes*, 1.11) asserts that we shouldn't seek to know when we die; it is better to have a drink and, while we talk, hateful old age will have fled.

Ovid (Roman poet, 43 BC–c.17 AD) – Ovid is notable in our story for the affection with which he wrote about the elderly. Although his love poetry gave him opportunities to rework the tropes of the old woman whom nobody honours by fighting over her, or leaving her garlands, he took time elsewhere (in *The Art of Love*) to praise the experience that the older lover can bring to erotic encounters. He also praised the simplicity and kindness of Baucis and Philemon, the old couple who were the only people to show hospitality to the gods Zeus and Hermes. Ovid had practical ways of keeping the elderly looking young, as his recipes for face-packs attest.

Plato (Athenian philosopher, c.429–347 BC) – Plato's thought is crucial to the philosophy that followed it, and this has direct implications for our understanding of old age and death. It is Plato's theory of forms, and the immortality of the soul, that Cicero finds so reassuring as he (through Cato) contemplates the end of life. As Seneca points out, it is Plato who argues that the things we can see don't really exist in the same way that ideas and abstractions exist, and we can appreciate these all the more fully when undistracted by our inferior, mortal senses. This can lead us to conclude that physical pleasures, which Cicero considers so damaging to our prospects of a calm old age, are transient and futile.

Plato also preaches the doctrine of respect for our elders. He does this particularly in his book *Laws*, in which he has speakers draw up plans for a utopian colony. Here, he presents parents as living gods, who should be venerated by their children. Elsewhere, Plato articulates his ideas through the figure of Socrates who, with his beard, wrinkly face and snubbed nose, usefully exemplified popular conceptions of old age: he could be stubborn, contrarian, and untroubled by the sound of his own voice, but also unarguably wise.

Plutarch (died after 120 AD) – Plutarch was a scholar and chronicler, who wrote in (elaborate) Greek and promoted Greek learning and culture. He was a towering authority on Roman history, too, and posterity (not least Shakespeare) owes much to his *Lives* – his sequence of biographies in which he paired Greek figures with Roman ones. His own treatise on old age, *Should the Elderly Run the Country?* (*An seni respublica gerenda sit?*), draws on Cicero's observations, and encourages older readers to take a greater role in public affairs.

Seneca (born in Cordoba, between 4 BC and 1 AD; died 65 AD) – Seneca was a playwright, statesman and philosopher. Having been Nero's tutor, he became powerful during Nero's reign, but distanced himself from his pupil as the latter's behaviour became ever more extreme. Eventually he was obliged to commit suicide, having been accused of being part of a plot against the emperor.

Seneca wrote often about ageing, particularly in his *Epistulae Morales* (moral letters), and also in his treatise *On the Brevity of Life*. His attitudes towards it varied, and some-times his letters can be read as a journal of how he feels at any given time. He thought and wrote extensively about suicide, sometimes arguing that it was worth leaving life if the mind was infirm, but also that it was worth persevering in the face of physical pain, which he felt could be over-come. His line of thought tended to be Stoic, but he was open-minded about Epicurean attitudes towards death, too. We examine his ideas further in section 7 below.

Solon (sixth-century Athenian lawgiver) – Solon helpfully divided the natural lifespan of a man into ten stretches of seven years each. He also introduced ways of challenging an old man's will in the law courts. The pithy utterance attributed to him in conversation with the Lydian king Croesus – 'Think no man happy until he is dead'– suggests a supremely virtuous attitude towards ageing, and allows for the idea that where there's life, there's always a chance for something to go horribly wrong. But his speech on this subject (mostly composed for him retrospectively by the historian Herodotus) does also praise the notion of making a good end, and that the best guarantee of happiness is a noble death (never minding that there's not so much time to savour the moment). As Cicero reminds us, it was Solon's old age that gave him the courage to confront the tyranny of Pisistratus in Athens.

Sophocles (Athenian tragic playwright, c.496–406 BC) – Sophocles would be worth noting for his own impressive lifespan, and a couple of anecdotes from him: in one, he thinks of old age as being a release from a desire for sex (as if from a cruel despot); in another, his sons try to declare that he is too mentally infirm to manage his own affairs, but he demonstrates his own powers to a jury by reciting lines from his work in progress, *Oedipus at Colonus*. That work is another reason why Sophocles is a notable guide to old age – it is a powerfully poetic meditation on death, age, the life review, legacy and dependency.

Zeno – the philosopher arrived in Athens in 313 BC, and studied there before founding his own school of philosophy, Stoicism (so called because he and his students met under the Stoa Poikile, or Painted Porch, in Athens). Stoics believed that the path to happiness was virtue, and that virtue lay in knowing how to interpret, and respond to, the logic, or reason, of the universe. This is what gives us the popular view of Stoics as people who gallantly accept their fate. The emphasis on virtue has a profound impact on Cicero's thinking (and later on Seneca's, if less reliably); for Cicero, a pleasant old age is one spent in the knowledge that life has been led virtuously. Zeno himself was especially quick to read the clues the universe was giving him about his plan: when he left his students and broke his toe, he assumed the gods were telling him his time was up, and to show his understanding of this, he held his breath and died.

THE ANCIENT ART OF
GROWING OLD

Introduction

Then the candidate [for archon] is asked whether he possesses an ancestral Apollo and a household Zeus, and where their sanctuaries are; next if he possesses a family tomb, and where; then if he treats his parents well, and pays his taxes, and has served on the required military expeditions.

Aristotle, *Constitution of Athens*

We're forever hearing about how the UK ranks in facing the problems all societies face. Are our children unhappier than anyone else's? Are they better at maths? And if there were a top 40 that listed our attitudes towards old age, where would we be?

We look to other cultures for an answer, and it's inconclusive. I have headed this chapter with a quotation from Aristotle, which may make us think that the Athenians were kind to their elderly citizens, and that we should therefore be the same; that a failure to look after one's senior relatives was shameful, and that this is still the case.

Does this logic work? 'The Indian government has even announced recently that it plans to name and shame people who abandon their parents.' Jeremy Hunt, the health secretary, offered this at the end of a speech about the steps his own government has been taking to make life for the elderly better – particularly for those in care.[1] It was full of odd statistics and some even odder deductions from them. He said that 400,000 people are in care, but 800,000 report that they feel lonely. (Do those figures have anything to do with each other? Are people in care lonely? The secretary of state didn't explore this.) He said that only 26 per cent of people surveyed said that they trusted the care system. (He said this round about the middle of the speech, perhaps hoping that his audience, National Children and Adults Services delegates, wouldn't notice too much. But outrages such as the abuse of residents at the Winterbourne View home in Bristol the previous year were strong in the memory.) He spoke of a need to make the running of care homes more transparent, and proposed that you could do this by covert filming. It's almost funny that the suggested means of ensuring transparency isn't at all transparent, and that Mr Hunt told his audience, 'Sunlight is the best disinfectant.'

Still, he reached an intriguing conclusion. It had little to do with the rest of the speech, but it was the part that attracted the most attention. In short, he argued that other cultures do a better job of looking after the elderly.

My wife is Chinese and I am struck by the reverence and respect for older people in Asian culture. In China and Japan it is quite normal for elderly parents to live with their children and their families . . . In those countries, when living alone is no longer possible, residential care is a last rather than a first option. And the social contract is stronger because as children see how their own grandparents are looked after, they develop higher expectations of how they too will be treated when they get old.

Critics were quick to pounce on this, and not just because it appeared to reinforce David Cameron's idea that we belong to a Big Society, in which we look less immediately to government to solve our problems, and to imply, if you want decent care for the elderly, do it yourself. Anthea Tinker, a professor of gerontology, said that the Asian reverence for elders is a myth, and that the world's largest care home – for 5,000 residents – is in China. One can't help feeling that China is big and diverse enough to help anyone prove anything from it. Islamic commentators were quick to find passages from the Koran to demonstrate that Muslims, too, offer a good example of how to honour our elders: 'Any young person who is kind to an elderly person because of his age, Allah will send him someone who will be kind to him when he becomes old.'[2]

We learn one thing from this: we don't know how well Asian cultures do on our imaginary list of positive attitudes towards the elderly. If the people of India are so attentive to the generations above them, why would their government need a law urging them to be better still? In looking at the records of lawmaking, we often have to ask if a law is there to reaffirm a society's values, or to address the constant violation of a society's best hopes. The example of China shows that even if we think we can gauge a society's values, generalisation is reckless. If some Chinese people are happy living with their parents, are there enough exceptions to warrant these burgeoning care homes? All of which leads us to the bigger question: can other cultures enlighten us, and even help us, when we contemplate our own old age and the ageing of those around us?

On the face of it, no. Different societies have different life expectancies, different relationships with technology, different expectations of what a welfare state can offer, different access to medical developments. Other cultures may resemble the UK in some respects, but by no means all. The UK itself is fragmented enough, with life expectancy for children born today ranging from 67 in one area to 105 in another.[3] That figure keeps changing in any case. And yet the problems and challenges of old age can seem unprecedented, given the demographic changes we can anticipate. For example, the number of people over the age of 80 living in the UK is predicted to double in 20 years' time. Our notions of pensions, of social care, of a happy, productive life, are taken to places we can't easily imagine.

With this subject in particular, one thing becomes clear from whichever culture we study: nothing is easy. If, as Bette Davis said, 'Old age ain't no place for sissies,' then we should become all the more interested in those communities that have found ways of making it more comfortable, honourable and even enjoyable. As we see the moment we open any ancient text, classical Greece and Rome were places where the plight of the elderly could often be remarkably horrible. So what use are they? The platitude 'There's always someone worse off than yourself' is never comforting, but there are moments when we can admire the attitudes of the ancients all the more for considering the trials they faced.

It's true that when an ancient writer raises his voice to instil optimism in those growing old, or to urge respect for the elderly, he's raising it because the tide of the debate is going the other way. Take the Greek orator Aelius Aristides, of the second century AD, who addresses the people of Rhodes about what an ideal state would be: people would marry whomever they want, education would be excellent, there would support for the poor, willing hospitality, and people would be looked after in old age.[4] As we will see, Plato, in his *Laws*, proposed legislation based on the assumption that parents should be seen as living gods, and venerated as such by children. But both Aelius Aristides and Plato, although writing 500 years apart, were talking about utopias – the implication being that their own worlds were nothing like this.

Still, they were asking the right questions. If students of our own society a millennium hence were to judge us on the strength of Jeremy Hunt's speech and on the success of Marie de Hennezel's *The Warmth of the Heart Prevents Your Body from Rusting,* along with the thoughts of opinion makers such as Joan Bakewell and Katharine Whitehorn, they might think that we had our problems, and that audiences and readers needed cajoling into a greater awareness, not only that it was time to give greater consideration to the elderly, but also that those who were not yet old needed to think harder about oncoming age. And yet I hope those students generations away would profit from the balance and sanity of those wiser souls who saw the situation clearly, and who articulated sensitive responses to it.

That is the aim of this book. It is to hear those voices that offered calm and even hopeful outlooks to the elderly, while having no illusions about the context in which they spoke. It is easy to dismiss this kind of effort as a sort of self-help book from the ancient world, an idea that strikes many as ridiculous. Tim Parkin, who has studied the plight of the elderly in antiquity more deeply than anyone, counsels extreme caution here: '[It is], I believe . . . a long-standing myth that in past cultures, both in antiquity and more recent history, older people enjoyed a life of prestige, comfort, and respect – with an implied contrast to the present day. That some did is certain. That most did not should be recognized.'[5]

And yet I stand by the title of *The Ancient Art of Growing Old*. To the ancients, 'art' meant skill, and a skill is something you need to learn. It is precisely because many of our sources feared age so much and ridiculed the elderly so freely that what antiquity's saner voices had to say sounds so urgent. Not everything is different. The young still have little conception of what it will mean to grow old; the old still have experience of a past from which the young can benefit; old and young together still struggle to define the extent of a life that is of use to society. However mythical or rare the practical examples of the ancients' best answers can seem, we can learn a lot from their own struggles to deal with the same problems in different worlds.

It's true that I want to focus on the more positive and elevating thoughts the ancients had about ageing, for obvious reasons; and when a Greek or Roman manages to confront old age while still maintaining a peaceful soul, he (always he) is facing severely negative attitudes towards the elderly, as well as the kind of infirmity that would have been so much worse in a world before medicine. While conceding that Tim Parkin is right, and that the idealised ancient world in which the elderly could expect piety from those around them is, if not mythical, then at best inconsistent, I still want to listen sympathetically to the writers who championed those ideals. In doing so, I accept that I can be accused of cherry-picking or making selective use of the sources in a way that risks misrepresenting the ancient world. I have two responses to this. The first is that we need to be clear-eyed about any horrors the Greeks and Romans faced, but what is really useful to us is some insight in how to overcome them. The second response is that classics as a discipline has recently developed in an exciting way to include the study of reception, which is to say, an understanding of how later generations have received the ancient world. So long as we remain sensitive to our own assumptions and requirements, we can hope to keep the discussion half-way honest.

For this reason, we sometimes pause in what follows to ask if we can take any lessons from the ancients. This enables us to consider comparisons between the old world and ours, although I have tried to avoid the feeling of the guidebook, with its chiding subjunctives: 'We should . . .' 'Let us . . .' My hope is that readers will have their own responses to what the ancients tell us, and don't tell us. As a result, what follows will sometimes be as much about us as about the ancients, and as much about new generations of the elderly as about older ones.

1

Looking back: How to make the most of the past

Perhaps you are old, or growing old, or can maybe imagine it. The first two can be hard, and so, in a different way, is the last: as Cicero says, old age is something 'which everyone wants to achieve, and which, once it's achieved, they rebuke'. But in each case it's worth asking: what advice is there for me? What can prepare me for the difficulties ahead? Need it really be so bad?

Inevitably, we turn to those who have been there before. But is that much use either? The conditions in which we are growing old change rapidly. My 65th birthday, if I reach it, will fall in 2036. At the moment 65 is retirement age, although at the time of writing the retirement age is set to rise to 67 from 2026. It's also the age at which my father died. That was from the consequences of multiple sclerosis, which stem-cell research will have made much more treatable by 2036. Treatments for cancer advance rapidly: although more people are likely to suffer from it, more are likely to find cures. The reverse is true of antibiotics, as illnesses become better at fighting them.

And then there's the life of the mind. We think about

senile dementia now more than we used to: as we live longer, it appears to affect more people, and even if it doesn't strike us, we still fear it. What about technology? It's not only medical invention that's changed our lives. My grandmother's grandmother must have had a tedious dotage without the benefit of television; or at least that's what I infer from my grandmother's own thoughts: 'If I didn't watch the cricket, the rugby, the tennis, the racing and the golf,' she once boomed at me, 'I'd be an awfully dull person.' Just at that moment I feared she was becoming one. She pooh-poohed my suggestion that I might read. 'Your eyes won't stand it.' But even if I were old, there'd be some drama from whatever the successor of Netflix will be by then, and more time to compose tweets undermining speakers on Radio 4.

My point is, the elderly today might be a good guide to how we might grow old tomorrow, but, at the risk of sounding like an impudent youth, they can't tell us everything – we have to find a lot out for ourselves. The world changes so rapidly, and the rate of that change continues to increase. What if we were to start from first principles? What if we were to seek the wisdom of cultures with no television, no printing and no knowledge of genetics, let alone any genetic treatments or understanding of antibodies?

At first, the exercise might seem to have limited value. Take the tenor of the anthropologist Jared Diamond's recent book *The World until Yesterday*. It asks what our modern world can learn from what he calls 'traditional societies', leading Diamond to apply his wide reading and experience, particularly in New Guinea, to our own societies. As he readily admits, it doesn't always work. If we take the elderly as an example, he admires 'the ways in which [traditional societies] have often provided satisfying lives for their elderly, a disaster area of modern American society'; but he must also recognise when some traditional societies are less ready to venerate the old, who are more likely to be seen as burdens if resources are scarce. Diamond quotes an Aché Indian from Paraguay, who says, 'I used to kill my aunts when they were still moving . . . I would step on them . . . I didn't use to wait until they were completely dead to bury them.'[1]

So what about the world of classical antiquity? Could this be any better? Well, we come across many of the same problems. It is impossible to say, 'The ancients thought . . .' about anything whatsoever. Their discussions about most things were personal, and even factional: would you have been a Stoic by temperament, striving to follow and accept the inherent logic of the universe? Or would you have been an Epicurean, and used your sensory responses to the world as a steer on what to do? Or would you have occupied one of the many possible positions in between these? Such questions make most matters murky, not least old age. It's true that certain trends emerge where a poet or artist is working within a particular tradition. For example, when a Latin love elegist derides an elderly woman, you can be sure he's doing it because someone else has done so. But when we read essayists on the subject such as Cicero or Plutarch, or the more medically detailed Aristotle or Galen, we come upon voracious and critical readers who take on all-comers and reach their own conclusions. The ancients may not have reached consensus, but they were, through their writings at least, in constant dialogue with one another, across areas and eras. Then add to this range of debate the difficulty with medicine itself. Depending on where you lived and whom you knew, your doctor could be anything from a well-read vivisectionist (where would you have been on the issue of experiments on humans?) to a faith healer or shaman.

Given this multiplicity of views about ageing, it's perhaps helpful to start by looking at the questions we ask about our own society, not least because we soon realise that we haven't come up with clear answers. Debates continue about the role of the elderly in society. Should they retire later? If they do, is that better or worse for their financial security or, more importantly, their emotional and mental wellbeing? And, once they do retire, how should we care for them? Should the state help with the costs? Should planning permission be relaxed so that more grandparents can be accommodated in the family home? Should they live in communities of their own? Should the upper age limit of jury service be raised from 70 to 75?

Many of these questions arise because our life expectancy is growing. Medicine is improving. The term 'quality of life' is so current that it has begun to sound like a human right, so that people strive to improve it or at least seek interventions when it dips. This leads to one of the most troubling questions of all: does there come a point at which life is no longer worth living? Should we prosecute those who take part in assisted suicide?

It's not always possible to find answers to these questions in the ancient world, and where we do, we'll find that their answers reveal how different their perspectives were from ours. For example, no ancient government would have commissioned the Hutton report on pensions, or the Dilnot report on care for the elderly. We will explore attitudes to those problems, but for now it's worth bearing in mind this, from the great ancient historian Moses Finley: 'There is not one text, to my knowledge, attesting either private or governmental action to assist the elderly – no charities, no pensions, no almshouses, poorhouses or old-age homes, nothing. Even the moralists did not go beyond an appeal for decent treatment and respect.'[2] As with pensions, so with other issues, to the extent that Finley concludes, 'One lesson of history, therefore, is that a study of how other eras coped, or failed to cope, with analogous problems may be an aid to reflection, but that we cannot find usable practical answers to our problems in the past.'

Finley's essay on old age is breezy and not his most brilliant piece of scholarship, but when it appeared it did have the virtue of identifying some valuable questions. At the time he didn't think there were answers, but subsequent scholars have come up with some impressive ones. As a result, we may not have usable answers, but there are more models that can aid reflection than Finley thought.

Now, Finley thought Cicero's treatise *On Old Age* a poor aid to reflection. I disagree: it's true that the socially progressive reader (such as Finley) may reasonably find its scant treatment of the real problems an old man faced unhelpful. There's almost nothing about diet, except for the advice to keep it moderate;[3] there's only the briefest mention of poverty, little about food supply, nothing at all about what it might be like to be an old woman, with the toll that child-rearing would have had; and most tellingly Cicero has this tick of using, sometimes in passing, the word *honoratus*. It doesn't completely mean 'honoured' – at least not in the sense of respected. Someone who's *honoratus* has been on the career ladder called the *cursus honorum* – the racetrack of public offices – and has something like a cabinet-rank CV to prove it. So the kind of old age he has in mind is that which we might imagine members of the say, Thatcher government enjoying: once fully engaged with running the nation's economy, and now avidly reading up on fracking to keep mentally active. It's one reason for the extensive name-dropping of consuls throughout the text.

All of which means that as we reflect on the ancients and old age below we'll be bearing Cicero in mind as a reminder that not everyone saw it that way – or at least that other views were available, given what we know about the ancient world. But, as Polonius says in *Hamlet*, 'By indirections, lead directions out.' Sometimes Cicero can offer off-key observations or appear to offer mixed messages about some sphere of old age: for example, anyone with an understandable concern for how he or she might enjoy sex in maturity will find Cicero a lot less helpful than Ovid, as we'll see. But his own perspectives along with his deep reading of other writers, particularly the Greeks, make him an invaluable go-to by whom, or against whom, to gauge the climate in which other ancients operated.

Before we start, it's worth examining an assumption that underlies almost all of what Cicero says in his treatise. As he puts it himself,

Bear in mind, though, that throughout this whole speech I am praising an old age that has been built on the foundations laid in youth (62) . . . that failure of strength . . . is brought on by the weaknesses of youth, because lustful, immoderate youth hands on a worn-out body to old age (27) . . . That's why I approve of the young person who has something of the elderly about him, and the old person in whom there's a bit of youth – because someone observing this might be old in body, but never in mind. (38)

It's worth dwelling on this for a moment, because it's as usable and practical as Cicero gets, and if *On Old Age* were to be a self-help manual, the message that would appear over and over again (with bullet points and sidebars of salutary examples) would be: start early. Is that so surprising a piece of advice? As we said at the start, if old age is hard, then so too is imagining it from a distance. An illustration of the difficulty is the Stanford marshmallow experiment. Researchers gave children a marshmallow each and then left the room telling the children that they could have two marshmallows if they hadn't eaten the first one after an interval of about fifteen minutes. Later on in life the children who could wait and earned the second marshmallow turned out to do better at school, as well as having better body-mass indices. The test has also been used more recently to promote pension plans.[4]

Cicero's thinking is the same. Plutarch endorses it when he argues that if you want to be an old person in public life, you shouldn't start too late, 'like some ignorant man who comes by at night ready for a party or a stranger changing not your address, or your country, but your way of life for one in which you have had no experience'.[5] There are, as it turns out, plenty of other tips for the elderly from antiquity that we will find familiar: keep your mind active, moderate your eating and drinking, keep exercising, don't be stingy. But by its very nature, this is the most urgent.

In calling this chapter 'Looking Back', I'm thinking not only of how we can make use of the historical past, but also of our individual life stories. Nobody these days is suggesting that to lead a contented old age you need to recall fondly your successful stint at the helm of a FTSE-100 company. But in 1963 the physician, gerontologist and psychologist Dr Robert Butler published a paper, 'The Life Review: an Interpretation of Reminiscence in the Aged'.[6] In it he argued that when the elderly appear to drift off into storytelling about the past, this is more healthy than unhealthy. It is, he argued, a 'naturally occurring, universal mental process characterized by the progressive return to consciousness of past experiences, and, particularly, the resurgence of unresolved conflicts'. According to Butler, the process can go either way: it could lead to what he calls 'personality reorganization' resulting in what Cicero would call a peaceful soul, or it could lead to anxiety. This anxiety is much more likely to afflict those who have suffered 'increasing contraction of life attachments'. Even if Jeremy Hunt's statistics are a strange succession of disconnected polls, it is still hard to deny that this affects a growing number of people, whom the health secretary called 'the lonely million'. Cicero has his own positive equivalent of this: 'The fruit of old age is the remembering and amassing of fine accomplishments.' A later writer, Favorinus, says that these are the things that old age can't take away from you. Plutarch articulates the flip side: 'Cato, for example, used to say that we shouldn't add the disgrace that comes from being bad to the many problems old age has already.'[7]

Robert Butler was more forgiving. 'Human beings need the freedom to live with change, to invent and reinvent themselves,' he wrote elsewhere.[8] Cicero was the expert at this. For one thing, he lived through the first stirrings of the most dramatic change in Roman history; as someone who liked to see himself as the saviour of the republic, he was dismayed by the way it effectively stopped being one under Caesar's triumvirate. For another thing, his own view of his achievements is as intriguing as the truth. He once wrote a letter to Lucceius, who was compiling a history of the times, with this nudge: 'And so I ask you outright again and again, both to praise those actions of mine in warmer terms than you perhaps feel, and in that respect to neglect the laws of history. I ask you, too . . . to yield to your affection for me a little more than truth shall justify.' In this way, at least, Cicero was a little easier on himself in practice than he could be on others in theory – if the life you're reviewing doesn't suit you, you can always adjust it a little. (One view of Cicero's philosophical writing, not least *On Old Age*, is that it was a reflection of his retirement and withdrawal from public life.)

This is another demonstration that we don't have to take the ancients prescriptively. We need do neither what they say nor what they do. But they are worth taking seriously. For example, this business of the life review, so evident in the career of Cicero and in his own representation of Cato, is a revealing glimpse at an impulse behind our own culture of celebrity – it is the fear of death and the need for something to survive us. Plato addresses the subject directly in his *Laws*, when he is considering the need to produce children as its yearning for a life beyond this one:

A man shall marry between the ages of thirty and thirty-five, considering that in a manner the human race naturally partakes of immortality, which every man is by nature inclined to desire to the utmost; for the desire of every man that he may become famous, and not lie in the grave without a name, is only the love of continuance. Now mankind are coeval with all time, and are ever following, and will ever follow, the course of time; and so they are immortal, because they leave children's children behind

19

them, and partake of immortality in the unity of generation. And for a man voluntarily to deprive himself of this gift, as he deliberately does who will not have a wife or children, is impiety. He who obeys the law shall be free, and shall pay no fine; but he who is disobedient, and does not marry, when he has arrived at the age of thirty-five, shall pay a yearly fine of a certain amount, in order that he may not imagine his celibacy to bring ease and profit to him; and he shall not share in the honours which the young men in the state give to the aged.[9]

Sometimes it can seem as if the ancients' preoccupation with their reputations and their need to have their accomplishments survive them accounts for the compulsive way in which many of them recorded their experiences and reflections, so that re-examining them in our own time becomes a kind of piety – in a good way. Seen this way, we are a young culture, forever changing and learning new tricks, listening to the words of another older one – older, not just in the sense of 2,000 to 2,500 years old, but old, too, in the valuable and vital sense of having a full, compelling and constructive engagement with its own past.

2

What was old age?

Ancient Greeks and Romans could live for a surprisingly long time. It didn't happen that often, though: it's been estimated that about 6 to 8 per cent of the population might have lived beyond 60, with 3 per cent passing the age of 80.[1] But the upper limits of the ages people could reach were barely lower than ours. These men and women, being fewer in number, were even less visible than in our own society, and the ancient population was as a whole much younger than ours. Our life expectancy continues to increase; theirs hardly did. It would be hard to prove that ancient Greeks lived longer than ancient Romans, but it often looks that way, especially from inscriptions.

According to the Office for National Statistics, life expectancy in the UK rose by four months between 2010 and 2011 (the age is 78.2 for men, and 82.3 for women); a boy born in 2011 is projected to have a life expectancy six years higher than a boy born in 1970; for girls it's eight years. Over a longer period the changes are bigger: at the start of Queen Victoria's reign (1837) the figure was in the high 30s, and 48 by the end (1901). The ancients wouldn't have experienced such dramatic rises – at least not over a sustained period of time, although in rural communities dependent on subsistence farming we can anticipate dips.

Life expectancy figures for ancient Greece and Rome are hard to establish exactly, but most estimates fall between 27 and 29. This may make the sight of an old man or woman a rare one, but the figures are as low as they are because infant mortality was so high. People would have looked old at a younger age than we do now, not only because of developments in cosmetics, but also in medicine. Garland thinks that for many in the ancient world the physical disabilities we associate with old age could have been obvious in your thirties.

Keith Hopkins, an ancient historian with a mastery of sociology and statistics, has estimated that 'more than a quarter of all live-born Roman babies died within their first year of life'; Robert Garland adds that 'about one-third of the children who survived infancy were dead by the age of 10'.[2] The richer could expect to live longer than the poorer, the urban longer than the rural. Karen Cokayne uses a model which suggests that a third of Roman babies would have died before reaching the age of one, with as many as half of all children dying by ten.[3] But once these hurdles were passed, the prospects were much better: Cokayne offers the probability that, once past ten, a child could reach 47.5 years. She finds the percentage of elderly people in Roman society close to the figure for Victorian England, between 6 and 8 per cent. (7.2% of the population in 1850 was over 60, she estimates.)[4]

Excavations at Olynthus, in the north of Greece, lead to more optimistic conclusions about children – in the cemetery there around 30 per cent of the bodies are of infants or small children. Admittedly, this isn't such a rural setting, and in any case we can't say exactly what class of people were buried here. We must also be cautious about the degree of accuracy with which this kind of research can assess the age at which long-buried people died. This science, called palaeodemography, has its problems and critics, and drawing precise conclusions from the study of remains is likely to be complicated if we're right to say that people showed the signs of old age sooner. Still, the dig did suggest a good chance of a decent maturity once people survived childhood. Scholars have similar reservations about the impressive survey by Bessie Richardson, who published an extensive inter-disciplinary study of old age in 1933.[5] She analysed 2,022 inscriptions from the Greek world on which an age could be found. Although funeral inscriptions, with their necessary literacy, are more likely to represent richer, healthier classes, the results are striking. The under-fives take up 11.52 per cent of the survey, and children from six to ten 7.27 per cent; the largest age group is 16 to 20 (at 14.54 per cent), which could be revealing in its own way. If, as we can infer from the Roman figures, youths were less likely to die at this stage, was a greater proportion of their deaths recorded because by then they had developed more of a personality? It is certainly fair to say that, given how frequently small children died in the ancient world, parents would have expressed less grief, although we can't speculate about what grief was unexpressed. Among the 18-year-olds in Richardson's survey we find 'Taapeis, daughter of Anoubion, teacher of gymnastics', and 'Aristokles, a hero'. This study is most surprising at its upper end. Five make it to over 100, and the oldest is Pancharius, father of the Elean synagogue, at 110.

Can we take these figures seriously? Did people exploit confusions about their date of birth to stretch their age? Possibly – on Roman tombstones, the letters 'PM' appear, standing for *plus minus* (more or less). When the ancient historian A. R. Burn analysed the data on Roman tombs, he found that 65 per cent of all the ages given were multiples of five. So we should be fairly cautious, at least about the details of longevity.[6] But Euripides died no younger than 75, and possibly at 79; Sophocles died either in his nineties or else very near them; Hippocrates could have died at 83, but probably lasted till 90 (100 seems as though his followers were advertising how good a doctor he was in practice as well as theory); the lowest date given for the orator Gorgias' lifespan is 105. Of the Romans, Cicero mentions the poet Ennius, aged 70, and the statesman Marcus Valerius Corvinus reaching 100. There could be many reasons why we hear less of aged Romans than Greeks, and Finley explores the idea that it was all in the wine: the Greeks used a resin to preserve it, whereas the Romans used a must, a *sapa*, which was simmered in a leaden vessel. (Finley cites a calculation that each litre of Roman wine could have contained 20 milligrams of lead.[7]) He apologises in case his argument seems frivolous, but remarkably the BBC reporter Andrew Bomford heard the same thing from a 98-year-old Greek man living on the island of Ikaria, where life expectancy is 10 years higher than in the rest of Europe. Over to Stamatis Moraitis (who thinks he might be older than 98, but anyway): "'It's the wine," he says, over a mid-morning glass at his kitchen table. "It's pure, nothing added. The wine they make commercially has preservatives. That's no good. But this wine we make ourselves is pure."'[8]

So when did old age begin? Pythagoras divided life into four phases, each of 20 years, with old age beginning at 60. Others took his sequence of numbers – 7, 21, 49, 56, 63 and 81) as being important markers in each stage of life, and called these years 'climacteric'. At 63 they anticipated a decline, including a mental decline. It was this age – the grand climacteric – that the emperor Augustus was pleased to have survived when he became 64. But there is little chance that this age reflected the physical, visible signs of ageing. Pliny the Younger writes of a consul, Q. Corellius Rufus, who was 32 when he first had gout.[9]

Solon assumed that we live for three score years and ten, and divided the time up into ten groups of seven years. (Solon died in 558 BC, at the age of 80.) Writers in the tradition of Hippocrates followed this approach. Here is how Solon describes them:

> A child throws out the first teeth that he's cut
> when he's still silly – in his seventh year;
> when God has given seven years more, the boy
> shows all the signs that mark him as a youth;
> and in the third, limbs grow, the chin has fleece;
> his skin shows it's adapting with a bloom.
> The following seven years are best – the signs
> of bravery and virtue show full strength.
> And in the fifth, a man's remembering
> to seek a wife, a legacy of children;
> and in the sixth, the man's mind is evolved –
> he less desires to do what he should not.
> His speech and thought are peaking at the seventh
> And eighth; he has both skills for fourteen years.
> He's competent in these come his ninth age,
> but speech and wisdom are both softening,
> and, should he reach the yardstick of the tenth,
> his turn to die will not be out of season.

You can see why a medic would have found this a helpful starting point; even the notes about speech are based on physical observation. What's more, each age is assessed for its social usefulness. In Solon's version the prime comes between 21 and 28 – the terms 'bravery' and 'virtue' suggest physical as well as spiritual courage – and yet there's a different kind of usefulness from 42 to 49. In this phase the once man of action becomes the counsellor, whose experiences make him worth listening to. If Homer's Nestor is a precedent, then the elderly adviser will have no end of vignettes from his own past. Even this faculty suffers from a decline that is physical. As Cicero has Cato say (perhaps in a reflection of Cicero's own situation), 'No doubt what charm the voice has can gleam in old age (who knows how); for sure, I haven't lost it, and you know how old I am. But still, a soft, relaxed tone befits an old man, and often it's that considered, gentle speech which makes people listen.'

This gives us some guidance on the key functions grown-up men were supposed to fulfil: youth was for fighting and the next stage for politics. These ages were defined differently by different people, and the transition into old age was never a matter of, say, reaching pensionable age. Roman law did identify 25 as the point when you reached your majority, and took control of your own affairs; for military purposes you were a *senior,* and not obliged to fight, at 46. But language makes distinctions where the law doesn't. The two stages of adult male life needed different words: *neos* and *gerôn* in Greek, *iuvenis* and *senex* in Latin. For women roles were identified differently: in Euripides' *Medea* the spurned heroine tells the chorus, 'I'd rather go to the front line three times than give birth once,'[10] a saying that's often taken as a delineation of male and female contributions to society. The archaeological evidence tends to support Medea: women could expect to die sooner, the hazards of their lives greatly increased by the requirement to produce children. If they could survive that, then they were more likely to outlive men, and as we shall see later, their roles in society are more apt to fit into mocked character types rather than any official function.

Still, Horace could send up the ages of man, too. He defines four – boys, young men, men, old men – and provides a sketch of each:

The boy knows how to talk and take assured
footsteps along the ground, plays with his peers,
rages and calms, changing from hour to hour.
The beardless youth, who's free at last from teachers,
revels in horse, hound, the parade ground's grass,
malleable into malice, scorns advice,
slack saver of provisions, free with cash,
loves the sublime, but bounds away from loves.
With different goals, the man's spirit and age
seeks wealth and contacts, slave to his career,
dreads doing what he'd soon struggle to change.
Bothers besiege old men, either because
they look for things they fear to use once found,
or else conduct themselves timidly, coldly,
skimp on long hopes, stay still but crave long lives,
are stubborn, testy, praising time they spent
when they were lads, chiders and scolds of youth.
The years bring many blessings as they come
and take them as they go. Lest we allow
young men to be old men, boys to be men,
let's keep to what is fitting for each age. [11]

Here Horace is taking his lead from Aristotle. At least Horace is talking about the different ages of man because he is advising writers on how to please different people. Aristotle gives the same advice to speakers, but confines his division to three phases. In his *Rhetoric* he characterises the 'youthful' character as driven by physical desires,[12] and, as Horace finds, those desires can change rapidly. He admires the optimism of the young, but finds plenty besides to which he can object: 'While they love honour, they love victory still more.' Aristotle finds even less to redeem old age. All that caution that's so useful to the state and all the moderation that Cicero preaches are just plain annoying to Aristotle. They're always saying 'possibly'; they 'think' rather than 'know'; and even the good impulses they have are for some bad reason: 'Young men feel pity out of kindness; old men feel it out of weakness, thinking that anything that happens to anyone else might easily happen to them.' In *The Warmth of the Heart Prevents Your Body from Rusting* Marie de Hennezel quotes a source who is frank about this touchiness.[13] She suggests that those characteristics which make the elderly seem difficult to the young are the very reasons why younger members of society should make more effort with the elderly: 'I would like to say to families: discuss things with your parents. It is their lives that you are manipulating. We are not toys. At our age, we take everything to heart; the merest thing can hurt us. So, if you please, do not regard us as puppets devoid of feelings as soon as we become burdensome.'[14]

With attitudes like this, we can see that the many consolations Cicero draws on to celebrate old age are prised from the enemy's hands, especially when the enemy reports them as scientific fact. (But then don't get Cicero started on a youthful approach to pleasure.)

Cicero's own division of life into sections is vaguer, and, while it is faintly disparaging about the earlier phases, retains the Stoic idea (as we shall see) that we should accept what life offers: 'The track of life is fixed; nature has one road, and it's direct. Each stage of life has its own season, so that childhood naturally has its dependency, youth its ardour, middle age its seriousness, and old age its maturity. You should welcome each in its time.'

There is a clue in Aristotle's rant that this is, if not physical observation, then at least medical deduction: 'Unlike the young, they have a temperament that is chilly.' It's a notion to which Horace refers with his word 'coldly' (*gelide*). This is the key to a more clinical explanation of what old age is. It's not as neatly parcelled up into age groups as Solon's seven phases are. And here archaeological remains are less likely to concur with the poet, at least if we take evidence from Roman Britain into account, where osteoarthritis was widespread: 80 per cent of the bodies found in Roman Cirencester had it among a population few of whom lived beyond 45.[15] The poetry of Juvenal is more than a match for these sober findings:

> There's little blood left in a frozen body[16]
> that warms only with fever; that's besieged
> by every kind of sickness . . .
> This one's shoulder's disabled, that one's groin,
> one's hip's gone; one, blind, envies the one-eyed;
> one's pallid lips take food from strangers' hands;
> and one, whose jaws would open at the sight
> of supper, waits now like a baby swallow
> whose starving mother flies full-mouthed to him.[17]

At any rate, it is even less possible to fix the rate of ageing than the age of dying. Seneca thought of old age as a disease in itself, and a list of ailments the ancients observed as afflicting the elderly includes urinary and respiratory problems, catarrh, kidney problems, insomnia and paralysis, ear and eye aches, bowel pains, dysentery and colic.[18] Aristotle saw the ageing process as a gradual cooling of the body. (For this reason, he thought people lived longer in hotter climates.) Ancient medicine was based on the idea that the body was governed by the four humours, each corresponding to an element: blood to air, yellow bile to fire, black bile to earth and phlegm to water. If the humours are unbalanced, you're thought to be ill, and as you approach old age, the humours are going to be unbalanced, especially if, as Aristotle says, ageing is cooling and drying. From this he concluded, like Seneca, that old age is an illness in itself – one which, as Seneca says, we cannot cure.[19] As Aristotle explains, 'Life must be co-incident with the maintenance of heat, and what we call death is its destruction . . . A small disturbance will speedily cause death in old age. Little heat remains, for the most of it has been breathed away in the long period of life.[20]

There is a problem with this theory: observing old people suggested to many ancients the opposite, they had if anything a surfeit of phlegm and spit. Galen, a later physician who did much to sort out the Hippocratic corpus of writings while conducting extensive research of his own, concluded that the outside of an ageing body might be wet, but the inner organs would still be drying. For Aristotle, this inner dryness was enough to cause death: 'the lung . . . becomes hard and earthy and incapable of movement, so it cannot be expanded or contracted'.[21] Galen took the basis of this thinking as his own starting point:

'This is why we grow old, some at one age, others at another, sooner or later, because we either are from the beginning by nature excessively dry, or become so either from circumstances, or diet, or disease, or worry, or some such cause.'[22]

None of which would be much use in a self-help book, especially if it's all so inevitable. Galen's thinking about all this, and how to maintain a healthy balance for as long as possible, has led many to turn to him as a champion of preventive medicine. For him too, old age was a disease, because it was a 'contra-natural' – a condition that militates against the body's health and is 'an inevitable infection of the body'. A recent article in the *Lancet* by Jack W. Berryman, a professor of bioethics, focuses in particular on Galen's advice on exercise as a way of staving off the onset of old age: 'the exercising body' results in 'hardness of the organs from mutual attrition [clearly less of a threat for Galen than for Aristotle], increase of the intrinsic warmth, and accelerated movement of respiration'.[23] But this respiration shouldn't accelerate too much – Galen was a believer in balance, after all, and excess was as bad as nothing.

For this reason, he urged his readers away from athletics, since the fierceness of the contest could lead to hyperventilation and, for that matter, 'miserable pain'. It's this that makes Cicero say, 'Let there be moderation in the use of strength, and let each man strive as much as he can – that way, he won't be afflicted by severe loss of it.' He follows this with a jibe at the bench-pressing cattle-carrying athlete Milo of Crotona.[24] In any case, the training regime involved over-exercising, over-eating and over-sleeping. As for horse-riding, boxing and throwing things – they're just plain dangerous and involve violent forces that are 'non-natural'

– external to nature. So what's the best form of exercise? He explains in his treatise *Exercise with a Small Ball*, in which he praises the game of *harpastum*, or snatching, because it exercises all parts of the body without too much risk.[25]

But one of the most useful, if vaguest, precepts we can take from Galen as we age is the fundamental Greek principle inscribed in the Temple of Apollo at Delphi, 'Know yourself.' Galen learned a lot from the study of his own youthful illnesses and hoped others would do the same. It was clear to him that each constitution was different, and he advised physicians to assess their patients according to their circumstances. The other maxim at Apollo's temple was 'Nothing in excess,' and this too can be taken as medical advice, especially if our fitness depends upon balance – not only of humours, but between action and rest, pleasure and restraint, emotion and reason. In these ways – getting to understand your body, and doing what you can to keep it fit – the best medical advice from the ancients is in keeping with the sagest moral prescription: start early.

Can we take anything from this?

Defining old age and its start – or 'onset', if, like some ancients, we think of it as an illness – is never easy. But it's interesting to note some harmonising between different voices on the subject. Here is Marie de Hennezel on turning 60: 'So I am officially entering my old age – my young old age, really, for I am in good health, active, and busy with a host of different projects. But, all the same, it is old age and, if all goes well, it will lead into extreme old age.'[26] And here is the classicist Mary Beard at 59: 'In fact some of these clouds [of old age] have silver linings . . . What is worrying is the thought of what might happen to us if we cross to the dark side, to the Tithonus side, of old age. Past the senior railcard, to a world of incapacity, indignity and incontinence.'[27]

For Beard, as for Moses Finley, it's money that makes the difference, at least to the first part of old age, which is 'still enjoyed by the relatively healthy and the relatively affluent (and affluence bolstered by decent pensions is, of course, crucial)'. Like Beard, Marie de Hennezel takes issue with the inadequate funds spent on care for the elderly. We will return to these problems (and these voices) later; for now, it's revealing that we do seem to be clearer about when old age begins. This is not only because of regulations about retirement and pensions, but also because of the medical conditions we most dread – in particular Alzheimer's, which affects more people as more people grow older.

We'll return to that, too, but for now, as we attempt to define old age, we simultaneously define our attitudes towards it. We could construct an irregular verb table to present the problem: I am mature; you are ageing; he is senile. But the younger among us can be more blanket than that – just as to a teenager anyone beyond thirty can seem past it, so we inevitably look at older people in the expectation of finding their limits. Can they still run? Can they still rumba? Can they still remember? So it's possible that we become more clear cut about our definitions than the ancients were: some of us are old; some of us aren't.

But it would be wrong to define old age by an increasing inability to do things. The best advice would seem to be, keep doing them. Where exercise is concerned, the advice from sports coaches as well as from doctors is, do it every day to maintain muscle tone. This at least is the secret of Ed Whitlock, the first man over 70 to run a marathon in under three hours. As Bupa's website explains, 'as you get older, your muscles get weaker, you tend to get more aches and pains, and become more prone to falls and injuries'.[28] The advice there is to do what suits you, but to aim to exercise for at least five days a week. 'The important point to remember, especially if you're just getting started and building up how much exercise you do, is to spend as little time as possible being inactive.'

This isn't saying that we should be in denial about growing old, but it is to say that we shouldn't use old age as an excuse to give up. Cicero may sound brutal when he has Cato remark that if we have a difficult old age, it's not old age's fault, but ours; and yet, why should we expect more infirmity and incapacity just because of some milestones? When old age begins may well be defined by the age of retirement, but even that is proving to be fluid, and the government must anticipate that we will respond by saying, 'All righty, let's keep working for another few years,' or a few more years than that by the time we get there. We may or may not appreciate governments that move the goalposts, or milestones, but we can at least agree with them, and with Plutarch, that we still have plenty to offer.

3

Looking old

If our definitions of old age confirm our own instincts or prejudices, then nothing's sure to make us leap to a conclusion about someone's age more than their looks. The world of advice available now on how to preserve the more visible ravages of old age is not just a matter of vanity – it's also about maintaining the appearance of being a vibrant and relevant member of society. The television presenter Fiona Bruce reminded us of this when she admitted to dyeing her hair, adding, 'I'm 48 years old and I feel very fortunate to be offered such amazing jobs. I know it's not always going to be like this. There comes a point – especially if you're a woman – when your career just falls off a cliff.'[1] It's troubling to contemplate the alternative: give it up. The ancient moralists did offer this advice, in practice as much as in theory – but then they were men too. But you don't have to be an ancient, or a man, to conclude that it's time to let it go:

> Were they really mine, those facial wrinkles, that sagging skin under the arms, that bald head, that flabby belly, those legs covered in varicose veins? How could we overcome

this sadness at the prospect of a withering body, and accept this damage to our self-image?

Without question, we must bid farewell to our bodies' objective beauty. Despite advances in aesthetic surgery, cosmetics, and public health, they will wear out, even if we play sport and watch what we eat.

That is Marie de Hennezel in her widely read book *The Warmth of the Heart Prevents Your Body from Rusting*.[2] Throughout *On Old Age*, Cicero says nothing about appearance. There's not even a mention of wrinkles or hair loss. The only physical change Cato registers in the speech Cicero gives him – apart from repeated mentions of less strength – is to his voice and, by extension, his lungs.

Is that because he's over it? Marie de Hennezel goes so far as to say, 'There's no doubt about it. We cannot escape this period of bereavement.' And the ancients were often in mourning. In his satire condemning any ambition for anything whatsoever, Juvenal shows how the pursuit of beauty will always be in vain:

Young people differ lots. One's prettier
than that, that than another, who is stronger –
old age has one face. Trembling voice and limbs,
a shiny head, and infant's runny nose;
his bread is mashed, poor man, by unarmed gums . . .[3]

It's certainly less likely that Cicero would have mourned the loss of his good looks, if he ever had them. For one thing, his sympathy with the Stoic philosophers explains the sentiment in his treatise, 'To those who look within themselves for all good things, nothing that the necessity of nature brings can seem bad. A prime example of this sort of thing is old age.' The line about nature helps him take facial wear and tear on the chin. Meanwhile, the thought that goodness comes from within sounds entirely modern, and in keeping with de Hennezel's qualification '*objective* beauty', 'Our narcissistic wounds will heal,' she writes, 'and then others will see another kind of beauty within us.'

Although he might have admired the persuasive rhetoric, Cicero is unlikely to have needed much of the persuasion. The fact is, he didn't care. He didn't have to. This is because of his gender, predictably, and less predictably because of his time. When Cicero was alive, wrinkly men could celebrate their wrinkles. At least, we can infer this from the style of portraiture called verism. Although the name suggests heightened realism, a sculptor in this tradition would go out of his way to exaggerate wrinkles, frowns and fine dryness lines. Faces ended up appearing so natural that in some cases later scholars have debated whether they are looking at a Roman *paterfamilias* or his slave. This representation wasn't the preserve of men either; a bust of a Roman woman from the first century AD shows that she, too, could appear unadorned, with pronounced bags under her eyes, but not undignified.[4]

There are two possible explanations for how this style evolved, and perhaps both had a part to play. One is the custom of the Roman household of putting lifelike heads of their forebears in their atria, which they would also carry in funeral processions so that previous generations would be able to say goodbye, or perhaps hello, to the deceased. Another is the earlier work of Greek artists in the Hellenistic period, which moved away from poised depictions of gods and heroes working through the set moves of myth, and towards a candid look at everyday life.

And here's where the differences between an old man and an old woman become more obvious. For example, there's the *Drunken Old Woman*, a Greek sculpture from the second century BC, of which there is a later Roman copy in the Glyptothek in Munich. The title is enough of a clue. We see her age in her veins, strung like cords as her neck strains to hold her head; and she holds the neck of the bottle in a way that can seem suggestive, at least if we compare it to the same image that Dutch genre painters used in their own language of symbols. And she's in tatters. You see the rags even if you go round the back of the portrait. The situation isn't much better for the old woman carrying a basket whose statue is in the Metropolitan Museum in New York. This too is a later Roman copy of a Greek original. Commentators think she is a prostitute. Why? Because she doesn't look poor: she's wearing a chiton (tunic), decent sandals and an ivy wreath. She appears to be going to a festival in honour of Dionysus.[5]

We can find old women in Hellenistic art who are going about their days without appearing set to walk the streets or roll in them, but the tendency is to portray elderly women as having suffered through some weakness the viewer could take to be moral. A genre of Latin poetry props up the stereotype: Roman poets are unsparing in their treatment of women. The brothel madame, called the *lena*, comes in for some especially harsh lines,[6] but so do others, often with the implication that looks will fade, and then who will be interested?[7] Here is Ovid in *Daily Mail* mode:

> Youth is for using; soon, though, it'll run –
> nothing that follows it will be as fun.
> In time, you too, who once rejected lovers,

will lie, a cold old maid, in lonely covers . . .
How quickly wrinkles wilt the body's frame;
lost is the hue that set a face aflame.
The white shocks you protest were always there
sprout suddenly throughout a head of hair.[8]

Given all this, a woman could be forgiven for applying a little rouge – who needs to mourn one's beauty when there are so many poets to do it for you? But ancient writers didn't approve much of this either. Ovid was an exception: he showed his support for the cosmetics industry by writing a verse lecture on how to prepare them, and why. His *Treatments for the Feminine Face* has a recipe for a moisturising face pack whose ingredients include honey, 10 eggs, 12 narcissus bulbs, gum, spelt, vetch and a ground-up hart's horn. Of another recipe, he assures his reader,

Before long, you must wipe the pack away
from your soft face; the colour, though, will stay.

Ovid sounds more practical, if a little tactless, about the matter of hair loss. The lawyer in him asserts that women are luckier with this than men:

Nature's kinder to women than to us.
You have so many ways to cover loss!
With men, hair snatched in old age will expose
   them,
as trees lose foliage when the north wind blows
   them;
women use German pigments to conceal
grey hair; the fake tint's better than the real.

It isn't thick enough? What do you care?
Go blow some cash on someone else's hair.[9]
Is buying wigs embarrassing? Oh please –
they're sold outside the shrine of Hercules.[10]

So when it came to baldness, not every man was as indifferent to his appearance as Cicero, who, if the busts of him are veristic, suffered from at worst a receding hairline. It took a special sort of writer, Synesius, of the Christian period, to write a rhetorical masterpiece, *In Praise of Baldness*, in which he takes the view that hair is overrated, is dangerous in a battle situation, and people with actual responsibilities tend to have little of it.[11] At Epidaurus, on the votive tablets on which people prayed for their illnesses to be cured, bald people often appear to want a miracle remedy. If Aristotle was right in seeing baldness as the result of an overcharged libido, you can sympathise. Using his theory of bodily dryness, he even accounted for why hair stays at the back of the head (there's no brain back there, so there's room for the moisture the hair needs to grow) and why hair around the temples goes grey (it's not at the really dry part, where the brain is, nor at that damp patch at the back, and so it's neither lush nor absent, just grey).[12] Martial is scathing in an epigram about a man who tries to conceal this:

Your hair dye lies, Laetinus – youth is gone.
You're swiftly raven – just now, you were swan.
You don't fool everyone. You're white. Just ask
Persephone, when she takes off your mask.[13]

Can we take anything from this?

The questions raised by the ancients about looks still tease us now. Are cosmetics the mark of a civilised society, as Ovid thought? Is trying to look younger than you are a kind of fib, as Martial reckons? Is it, after all that, an unnecessary fib, and should we do as Cicero says by looking into ourselves for all good things?

In 1998 *Vogue UK* featured a debate about women and ageing.[14] One participant, the GP Susan Horsewood-Lee, said, 'I feel that everyone's intrinsically beautiful and it's things like pain, grief and anger and other problems that make it evaporate.' If that's the case, then Cicero's guide on how to prepare for an old age that's light on resentment, regret, envy and indolence can claim to offer support here. Others in the discussion affirmed this faith in 'inner beauty', but *Vogue*'s then beauty director, Kathy Phillips, was franker: 'Well, I have to say that it's an irony to listen to us all sitting around saying it's great to be older when I know that the phones are ringing in the beauty department with women our age asking, "Where can I get botox injections? Do you know who I can have my face lifted by?"'[15]

For Ovid, an ability to use technology is what separates the kind of sophisticated society he loved from the kind of crude society for which his ruler, the emperor Augustus, hankered. Ovid mocked the hardy Sabine women for their wrinkles and lack of make-up and, as we've seen, he patented his own face-pack recipes. If everyone is applying this kind of technology (*cultus*, Ovid calls it) then it becomes ever harder to grow older naturally when so many are seeking cosmetic intervention – and at an ever-younger age. Fay Weldon brought this up in the debate, in connection with her own facelift: 'I felt fine. I did notice that because they're mostly done by men, you get the strange sense of being recreated with a masculine vision of beauty – being told that this plastic surgeon has done all these people, and this is what he thinks you should look like, so therefore this is all right.'

This mutually assured reconstruction makes it more likely still that we will say, 'You look great for your age,' rather than, 'You look great because of your age.' Nick Knight's accompanying photographs somehow allow for both possibilities: there is no sparing of light (or at least he's using art to conceal the art), and all but one of his models, aged from 52 to 100, smile.

This seemed bold as recently as 1998; now, to convey the glories of old age with a photograph of a 52-year-old woman is to make no point at all. In 2014 *The Times* journalist Hilary Rose wrote that there is a growing number of older models, reflecting the needs of a growing elderly population, and what they mostly advertise are anti-ageing products.[16] But there's a paradox: to do this, you have to look old enough to use it but beautiful enough to have had the benefit. The message seems to be, grow old naturally, but not *too* naturally. Know yourself, but don't do too much.

Rose spoke to three prominent models – Daphne Selfe (85), Jan de Villeneuve (70) and Pam Lucas (68), and concluded, 'All three share a matter-of-fact approach to getting older: no plastic surgery, regular exercise and good although not necessarily expensive skincare. They make some concessions to what they wear, but as de Villeneuve says, "You're not going to look 27 again. You can't go backwards."'

This affirmation of moderation and honesty would appeal to Cicero as much as the anti-ageing products would appeal to Ovid. But in their time the elderly were much smaller in number, and, as some have argued, lived more on the margins of society and the extreme end of experience. And then they had less of the science. So, given the range of problems the ancients faced and the rapidity with which blemishes stole upon them, there are two attitudes we can adopt when we confront our ageing faces in the mirror:

1. Think of how much worse it could have been if you were living in the ancient Mediterranean.
2. Make a thing of it.

4

Old loving

What you don't miss can't bother you. When he was an old man, Sophocles put it well when someone asked him if he still enjoyed sex. 'Good heavens! I've run away from that, as if from a crude and raging master.'

Cicero takes this story from the start of Plato's *Republic*. It's a good story, but one that works less well today. The assumption that elderly people don't want sex is an offensive one, all the more sinister because an assumption is all that it is, rather than a discussion. Still, the more the elderly claim their right to be considered as enduringly sensual, the more balanced a discussion can be.

We can't simply say that old people lose their desires. In fact, we simply can't say it. It's possible that some might want not to want, but the most poignant reflections on desire come from those who still feel it. As Thomas Hardy puts it in his poem *I Look into My Glass*,

> I look into my glass,
> And view my wasted skin,

And say, 'Would God it came to pass
  My heart had shrunk as thin!'

For then, I, undistrest
  By hearts grown cold to me,
Could lonely wait my endless rest
  With equanimity.

But Time, to make me grieve,
  Part steals, lets part abide,
And shakes this fragile frame at eve
  With throbbings of noontide.

In the late seventh century BC, the elegiac poet Mimnermus expressed something similar:

Without love's goddess, where's pleasure?
  Where's life?
Please may I die when I have had enough
of bedrooms, sweet gifts and illicit love.
These blossomings of youth's enchantment thrive
in women as in men. But when old age,
so hateful, gives a man an ugly face,
and chafes at him to make his instincts base
so that he'll menace young men and outrage
women, and even sunshine leaves him cold –
then god imparts the grief of growing old.[1]

But then there's Cicero – and there's his mouthpiece Cato. Plutarch tells us that Cato married in old age, and when Cicero was 60 he married his young ward, having divorced his wife, to whom he had been married for 29 years. Both men would have recognised the noontide throbbings.

All this helps to make Cicero's own approach to the matter of love and sex comically awkward. He castigates pleasure – *voluptas* – in the same way he would take a defendant to the cleaners in his glory days as a prosecutor. When he was consul, he argued that everything bad that happened in Rome was somehow the fault of the conspirator Catiline, and in later life the villain is pleasure: 'This is where treason and revolution are born, and conspiracy with the enemy; ultimately, there is no crime, no evil deed that the lust for pleasure hasn't provoked. That's right: rape, adultery and every offence of that type are incited by nothing but the temptation of pleasure . . .'[2]

But, as if Cicero is attuned enough to how his speaker might sound, he has Cato make an accommodation with pleasure – a confession that he used to enjoy 'early dinners'. These were dinners that people would begin before the acceptable time of about 3 p.m., so that festivities went on all the longer for having started before the end of the working day. As a result, 'early' or 'timely dinners' became a byword for decadence. And then there's the extraordinary passage in which Cato extols the more seemly joys of bringing crops to fruition. (Ovid has a similar passage in *The Cures for Love*, in which the besotted reader is advised to sublimate his sexual desire by a retreat to the countryside.) It feels schoolboyish to titter at how Cicero uses words that have erotic meanings in English – *semen, vagina, erecta, pubescens*. What's more, the earth is personified, accepting all this seed into its lap.[3] Cato is so obviously talking about sex that it becomes a clever piece of rhetoric, and the speaker avoids having to say, 'Does that make agriculture sound fruity enough for you?'

It captures more than the awkwardness of talking about sex, a subject about which few Romans were coy, including Cicero, who acknowledged that we share with animals the desire for procreation (*libidinem procreandi*), and that it is the seedbed of the state (*seminarium reipublicae*).[4] Rather, in turning the speaker's own passions towards horticulture, it also captures the awkwardness of talking about elderly sex, a subject which has even Horace sounding like less than his genial self.

The real horror for a man of classical times is the idea of a woman with desires, particularly an elderly one. Aristophanes is especially harsh in his treatment of them. His play *The Women of the Assembly* offers a dystopian view of how Athens would be if women made the rules, and one edict on which the elderly insist is that if a man wants to have sex with a young woman, he has to have sex with two old women first. (The dramatist draws this joke out to fill about a sixth of the play.) We have already seen the statue the *Drunken Old Woman*, and noted how undesirable an artist could make desire look.

The prurience around the subject of an elderly woman's passion has stuck stubbornly since ancient times. This in itself makes classical attitudes worth knowing about: anyone still uncomfortable with the idea is still the heir of ancient thinking, and if you want to take a more progressive approach to feminine desires and geriatric sex, it helps to know the enemy. Chaucer's Wife of Bath is a particularly puzzling example of how this debate has continued. Her own declamation against the misogynists of classical times and the early Christian Church is so imbued with jokes about women's desires that she ends up laughing at herself (or is that Chaucer laughing at her?):

> It tikleth me aboute myn herte roote.
> Unto this day it dooth myn herte boote
> That I have had my world as in my tyme.
> But age, allas! that al wole envenyme,
> Hath me biraft my beautee and my pith.

> Lat go, farewel! the devel go therwith!
> The flour is goon, ther is namoore to telle;
> The bren, as I best kan, now moste I selle . . .[5]

But not everyone was so appalled by the idea of sex among the elderly. At least, with qualifications, we can take Ovid as an honourable exception (with the caveat that, if the ancients seldom agree with each other, Ovid can't be relied upon to agree with himself):[6]

> Don't ask her age, or who was head of state
> when she was born (let censors keep the date),
> especially if her youth has passed, bloom fled
> and now she plucks white hairs out of her head.
> This is an age (or later) youths should know –
> the field is fruitful; it's a field to sow . . .
> What's more, they have more wisdom in these things;
> only they have technique experience brings.
> They compensate with knowledge of the world
> and take some trouble not to seem so old,
> so you can choose one from a thousand ways
> to have sex – more than any book displays . . .
> These are the benefits nature deprives
> from most, except the over-thirty-fives.
> Let those who want to rush drink Beaujolais –
> pour me the wine that's long been put away . . .
> Between Hermione, or Helen, her mother,
> Medusa and her mum, whom would you rather?[7]

He manages to praise the older man too, who is less violent and more enduring:

He burns slowly, like hay before it's dried
or timber fresh-felled from the mountainside.[8]

There was less mockery of old men, so libidinous and so
bald, but it was there: Roman theatre-goers were used to the
stock figure of Pappus, the grandfather figure, 'with special
emphasis on the old man's sexual, though impotent, proclivities'.[9]
Even so, the Benny Hill figure attracted less stigma than the
jibes at the desires of old women. It helped that men enjoyed
higher social status, particularly if they had led a public life. Just
as Cicero and Cato had had little difficulty in finding a younger
wife, so Pliny the Younger was able to brag about his own
younger third wife, who, he says, loved him for his reputation.
So a distinguished past was an advantage to an ageing man, and
brought with it not just happy memories of his career.

Men had it easier for other reasons too. In Athenian
society older men consorted with younger men – often
barely or not even men – and this was justified as being
good for the youths involved. In a speech in *The Symposium*
that Plato gives to Aristophanes it even sounds like
networking. Men did have a duty to produce children for
the good of the state, but, unlike in post-Christian societies,
this was far from the only purpose of sex. Greeks would
still worry about adultery, but this was linked to the idea
that a man's wife was his property, and no one else's.[10]

So men were more likely to lament the loss of desire
rather than the loss of opportunity. This would have had a
knock-on effect for women, especially if they remained
married around the time of their menopause. However
funny the ancients found the idea of an ageing woman
wanting sex, there is every reason why this should have
been a regular, painful and repressed reality.

It was a common fate to be a widow, since, as we've seen, mothers who survived childbirth were likely to outlive their husbands. They were also much younger than their husbands: whereas a man might wait until his late twenties or early thirties to marry, his bride was all the more desirable for being at the beginning of her fertile life, the early to mid teens. The laws passed by Augustus Caesar to protect marriage and to promote the birth rate among Roman citizens indicated that men were not expected to father children at the age of 60, nor women to give birth after the age of 50. The emperor Justinian was consulted about this, and replied, 'We decree that, although a birth of this kind is extraordinary and rarely occurs, nevertheless nothing which is known to be plausibly produced by nature should be rejected.'[11]

Losing your fertility was always difficult: ancient doctors considered the menopause to be an especially troubling time, and that's before we start considering the social stigma. But it was no easier *not* to have lost your fertility: for a woman to be single, but considered fertile, was to invite suspicion. Women could remarry once their husbands had died or divorced them, but as the ancient historian Nancy Demand says, 'A single life for a woman still capable of childbearing, whether as widow or divorcée, was considered pitiable.'[12] Pericles was especially concerned about them during the Peloponnesian War: 'If I am to speak of womanly virtues to those of you who will be widows from now on, let me sum them up in one short admonition: For a woman not to show more weakness than is natural to her sex, and not to be talked about among men for good or for ill, is a great glory.'[13]

Montaigne took this a step further: his essay 'On Glory' argues that women have no need to worry about honour because it tells us nothing about their intentions and desires, which should be as well regulated as their actions.

These burdens on widows demand that desires felt between childbirth and any loss of desire should go unfulfilled; worse still, Pericles' words 'than is natural to her sex' actually invite the assumption that a woman will feel those desires.

Can we take anything from this?

Many ancients repeatedly maintained that old men lose their desire and that old women's appetites, where visible, are disgusting. We know that neither of these things is true, and some of the ancients did too. Ovid recommended the love of an older woman; unlike Sophocles, Mimnermus didn't want to lose his appetites and thought his life would be as good as over without desire. It's even possible that the end of life increases desire: as the novelist Elizabeth Jane Howard, then aged 89 and in her last year, told Louise Carpenter, 'I sometimes ask myself, "Would you really want someone in your life?" And when I think I would the person is absolutely perfect and fitting in with me all the time . . . But in real life, am I up to the rough and tumble? The arguments? I think I am really!'[14] Marie de Hennezel's chapter 'A sensual old age' finds silences about an elderly woman's libido even today, but the author thinks things are changing because of the baby-boomer generation, who have known contraception: 'They are not ready to give up on physical love as they grow older, and scientific progress is helping them.' She also finds men and women who experiment with ways of intercourse that spend a prolonged period building towards climax without releasing it.

The reality is that old people do experience desire and are prepared to invest in the time, and even the technology, to allow them to fulfil it. Whether new technology can help the elderly make love or not, it is better to fear failure than ridicule.

But are we quite ready for that? The *Daily Mail* in 2014 ran stories on Susan Sarandon and Jacqueline Bisset, each allowing the reader to marvel that these women were still able to lead racy lifestyles at the respective ages of 67 and 69.[15] Sex is one of the areas in which the ancients were harshest about old age, and yet we seldom come closer to their attitudes towards the elderly than when we're thinking about sex. Medea rescues Jason, who leaves her for a younger woman; she becomes the type of the scorned, vengeful lover – if we call her a bunny-boiler, we can see how little distance we've travelled between the *Medea* and *Fatal Attraction*. Meanwhile the link between older men and younger women finds a formal expression through the existence of 'sugar-daddy' websites, in which old, richer men help young women with their student debts. One administrator of an American site said, 'Sex isn't expected, but it can be aspired to.'[16] Here again the comments of Pliny the Younger about his trophy wife put us in a world from which we haven't always travelled so far. When we look at the relationships of others, we will naturally make our own judgements; as we do so, a glance back at ancient attitudes towards old people in and out of love will continue to help us understand the frameworks that have shaped our own responses to love, sex and the elderly.

5

The old in the home and the community

So far the prospects for us have looked better than for the ancients (even in the bedroom), but when it comes to the contrast between how our different cultures care for the elderly, we may start to wonder. This is the area that worries us the most, and worries most of us. Will we be a burden on our families when we are old? Will we be able to look after our parents? Are we caught in what has been called 'the sandwich generation', struggling to make our lives work between ageing parents and little children?

I said earlier that there would have been no Dilnot report in the ancient world on how to care for the elderly; there would have been no need. It was assumed that the children would grow up to take care of the old. This assumption was fundamental to how ancient societies worked. In the *Iliad* a hero dies, and Homer remarks that the fallen warrior can no longer have the honour of looking after his parents as they grow old:

> He couldn't give
> his parents' nursing back – he was short-lived,
> killed by big-hearted Ajax's conquering spear.[1]

For a moment, a war narrative pauses to reflect that there is a sort of glory different from dying for your country.

The word for this caring is *threpteria*. It's hard to translate, but any rendering would have to carry the implication of nursing, because *threpteria* has its roots in *trephein*, 'to nurse'. This reflects how a child becomes an adult and is capable of doing for his parents what they did for him.

Although there were no reports into any problems arising from this, the custom was fundamental if not always followed. Solon had to pass a law to ensure that Athenians observed it, on pain of losing their citizenship. The condition was that the parents had to have given their children a trade. As we have seen, the Athenian council and law court would examine candidates for the office of archon, and one question was, 'Do you treat your parents well?' Plato's last book, *The Laws* (finished in the early 340s), is a dialogue in which men proposing to start a colony on Crete discuss how to run it and by what values. Given the nature of the project, it's hard to tell when Plato is asserting a value that prevailed in Athens, or one that he wanted to try out on his readers. In either case, a speaker meets with no dissent when he says,

We must reckon that the most precious object of worship a man can have is his father or grandfather, weak with age, or his mother in a similar condition, because when he honours and respects them God is delighted . . . These 'living shrines', in the shape of our forefathers, affect us far more wonderfully than lifeless ones, because when we look after them they invariably join their prayers to ours, whereas if we insult them, they oppose us . . . a good man will regard his elderly forebears as a veritable god-send, right up till they breathe their last.[2]

The punishment Plato proposes for failure to do this is whipping and imprisonment for a man if he's under 30, and the same for a woman if she's under 40. This suggests that some needed coercion to fulfil their duties. The poet Hesiod, writing in the eighth century BC, considers it characteristic of the degenerate people who live in his era – not the age of gold, or even silver, but of iron:

> Fathers will row with children; vice versa . . .
> Children won't honour their senescing parents,
> but blame them, come to them with nasty words,
> the fools, not seeing the gods will punish them.
> They won't make recompense to the ageing parents
> who reared them . . .[3]

This rivalry between generations is a situation that Greek dramatists repeatedly addressed. Plato alludes to two stand-offs between father and son from myth: when Oedipus curses his sons, and Theseus curses Hippolytus, the gods automatically side with the parent. This didn't stop both tragic and comic playwrights exploring the tensions that arose. An example that's shocking enough now, let alone to a Greek audience, comes from Euripides' play *Alcestis*. When Admetus learns that he can live for ever if someone is prepared to die in his place, his parents decide they aren't, and without telling him his wife Alcestis gives her life on his behalf. Admetus bans his father from attending the funeral, and adds this:

> And all a man requires to feel he's blessed
> you have: when you were young, you were a king;
> I was a son to you, heir to your house,

so you would not be childless and bereft,
about to leave your house for others to snatch.
You surely can't say you'll abandon me
to death – I've not dishonoured your old age:
I showed you real respect, and what a favour
you and my mother do me in exchange!
So you should hurry – you no more have children
who'll feed you when you're old, who'll swaddle
    you
when you are dead, and who'll put out your corpse.
No, my own hand will never bury you,
because to you I've died. And if I find
another saviour and still see the light,
I'm their child – when they're old, I'm their dear
    nurse.
It's pointless when an old man prays to die,
whining about old age and life's great length:
nobody wants to die when death's at hand;
no, old age isn't such a burden yet.[4]

The chutzpah is breathtaking, and we fully anticipate that Plato's legislators will whip Admetus soundly: he appears to expect such credit for staying alive, as though that in itself were an act of devotion when in fact it's something he'd love to do anyway, even without a father. But, outrageous though he is, he still clings to the language of honour: 'carer' might be better than 'dear nurse', but in the Greek *gerotrophon* the 'troph' root that we saw in *threpteria* comes back. 'To feed the elderly' is just one word in Greek – another demonstration of how established these concepts are, even in the mind of Admetus.

It should be said, though, that the verb he uses – *geroboskeo*

– has overtones of providing for livestock. If that makes the treatment of the elderly seem like animal husbandry, it can work both ways. Tim Parkin ventures a comparison with the difficulties exposed by our own welfare state, in which the populous, thriving generation created by the baby boom is coming to rely on the less numerous children it spawned for its pension provision:[5] 'the phenomenon of childbearing as a form of old-age security in various modern societies has increasingly become a renewed object of investigation. It has been discovered, indeed, that over time fertility levels often increase in such societies.'

In Aristophanes' *Clouds*, a son who's been to Socrates' sophistry school hits his father repeatedly over the head and seeks to justify himself by using warped arguments. At least they might have seemed warped to an audience alarmed by a boy striking his father, no matter how accustomed they were to role reversal in comedy. But the son's response plays with another understanding the audience was able to share: 'How come your body must be free from beatings, but not mine? Children cry, and you don't think it's right that a father cries? You'll say it's laid down in law that this is the role of a boy; but I riposte that old men are boys twice over: it's better that old men cry than young men do, seeing that it's more wrong for them to make mistakes.'[6]

The idea of the old living a second childhood is familiar; it's what makes *threpteria* work. They need nursing. But the son explores difficult territory: what happens when the father – the lord (*kurios*) of the house – makes mistakes? Is there room to question his responsibility? We will consider memory and mental well-being below. For now it's enough to note that such clashes happened and needed addressing.

In Roman law it was understood that children would help their parents – or at least their fathers – but this was something a judge would have to decide, depending on the means of the offspring and the needs of the parent.[7] The default position for the Roman family, especially in imperial times, was that the father was the emperor of the family, just as the emperor was the father of the nation. The oldest man in the family assumed this role. In Athens a law introduced by Solon maintained that a man's will was valid unless he was insane, senile or impaired by pain, violence, drugs, dementia or 'the influence of a woman', and as a result wills were often challenged in the courts. If the appeal was successful, the old man could be compelled to assume the status of a child. In Roman law it was possible for a younger man to demonstrate that his father was no longer able to administer his own affairs and for the son to take over that responsibility, and yet, even though the son could become the father's *curator*, the father was still *paterfamilias* in name.

As in Athens, so in Rome – this relationship was the butt of the dramatists' stock jokes. It was from the Greek comic playwright Menander (and to some extent Aristophanes himself) that Plautus and Terence borrowed the character types of the dotty father and the impulsive son, one better at retaining money than the other. The flow of cash from one generation to the next was always going to be a problem, which explains the frequency of legacy hunting. Horace wrote an ingenious satire in which the still-living Odysseus goes to the underworld and meets the beyond-old (because long-dead) Teiresias. Odysseus fears that his kingdom will have been depleted by suitors on his return, so Teiresias gives him advice on how to make up the shortfall by wangling shares of wills:

> Another pointer: if the grieving wife
> or freedman sways the old and crazy man,
> become their ally.[8]

These jokes reflect the regularity of gold-digging, but also to some extent the grip the elderly had on cash. Aristotle complains the old are ungenerous, and it's one of the few points concerning age on which Cicero agrees with him: 'And what avarice in the elderly can achieve, I really don't understand. Is there anything more absurd than the traveller who looks for more luggage when there's little of the journey left?'[9]

In ancient Athens there was a more civilised way of ensuring an inheritance from someone outside the family: you could adopt one. Isaios described this kind of adoption as 'the only refuge against isolation and the only possible consolation in life for the childless'.[10]

The issue of money leads us to the question: how dependent were the elderly on the rest of society? This isn't quite like asking about the need for a working population to contribute to the next generation's pensions, but it is surprising just how often old age and poverty are linked, even by metaphor.

Moses Finley says that financial provision for the elderly gets just nine words in Cicero's *On Old Age*. Actually, it isn't quite that bad – Cato brushes the question aside with an anecdote and only briefly concedes that money is much worth worrying about. His interlocutor says to him, 'Perhaps someone would say that your old age seems more bearable to you because of your wealth, resources and standing; but for many people that can't be the case.' After an anecdote, Cato says that old age 'can't be easy even for somebody wise if they're in a state of utter destitution, and can be severe to fools even if they enjoy the height of affluence'. Later, he namechecks the poet Ennius, who at 70 was said to have lived in poverty as if born to it. The best defence, he says, is virtue, to which many readers might say, 'Thanks a lot, Cato.'

So *was* there any provision for the elderly within the classical community? Finley admits he couldn't find any. Before him Bessie Richardson had expressed the hope that 'a people of so high a degree of culture' as the ancient Greeks would have co-ordinated some support: 'We note the absence of friendly societies established for provident and benevolent purposes, and institutions for the care of the aged, and pensions, but it is likely that contributions were made by friends for these purposes as the need arose.'[11] (Ancient Rome did have burial societies, often organised by people in the same guild or trade.) The ancient historian, the late Thomas Wiedemann has looked harder for examples of community support, especially in the Roman world,[12] and asked a tricky question that takes us to the other end of society: what would have happened to old slaves? Quite often, at least in cities, they would have been given their freedom, especially if they were part of a household. Cicero himself was an encouraging example, because he freed his scholarly slave Tiro and bequeathed him an estate in his will. (Tiro quite possibly lived to be 99.) Pliny the Younger gave his old nurse 100,000 sestertii. But this was more the way of the urban elite, and would have been much less likely in rural communities, where slaves worked on large-scale farms and had a much lower life expectancy, with hard labour adding to the disadvantages of poor care and restricted diet.

So what about those slaves, who were on the lowest rung any social ladder could have? Cato (yes, Cicero's Cato) said that you should sell an old slave, a sick slave and any other survivor. This raises the question: to whom could you have sold them? In any case, it's advice that reminds us that slaves were often no use, especially past 60. The emperor Diocletian went as far as to say that slaves were worth 15,000 denarii, except those aged younger than 8 or older than 60 (10,000 denarii).

Wiedemann provides a range of suggestions. Some perhaps helped at temples, where a community of worshippers could have contributed to their needs. In AD 47 the emperor Claudius passed a law that prohibited owners from leaving their slaves on the Tiber Island. Giving succour to slaves was a practice more often discussed in the Near East than in Rome, but it happened in Rome too. Some begged – or rather, went about the streets offering things no one really wanted in exchange for money: Juvenal shows us an elderly Jewish woman who will interpret your dreams in whatever way you want for small change. (The change is small because these tailor-made readings are necessarily unreliable.) We rightly worry about the insensitive and inflexible tests people take now to qualify for disability allowance. In ancient Rome these matters were more ad hoc: if you could prove that a beggar was claiming he wasn't able to work when really he was, you could make him your slave.

The very luckiest slaves could have been freed early and saved for later life; some might even have been paid. But not all slave owners were rich – quite a few had been slaves themselves – and not every slave had a Cicero or a Pliny for a master. If there was a net through which old slaves could have slipped, they would have done, but there was no question that public money could provide any net. When Pliny was a governor in Bithynia, he found that he was landed with people who had been sentenced to death but had then been made slaves instead. Many were now too old to work, so he wrote to the emperor Trajan for advice. Trajan replied that they should go back to menial jobs or else face the original sentence of execution. But public money was unthinkable: it would be 'to feed the idle [*otiosos* – "leisured"] pointlessly'. In ancient Athens there are hints that there were slightly better futures. When Pericles heard that an ageing slave had broken a leg, he said, 'There's another teacher.'

Given the likelihood of financial hardship, it seems especially harsh that the elderly in the ancient world should have acquired a reputation for meanness. Aristotle sees it in black and white: 'They are not generous, because money is one of the things they must have, and at the same time their experience has taught them how hard it is to get and how easy to lose . . . Their sensual passions have either altogether gone or have lost their vigour; as a result, they don't feel their passions much, and their actions are inspired less by what they do feel than by the love of gain.'[13]

This is in contrast to the young, who Aristotle says prefer honour and victory to money, hence Horace's line, 'slack saver of provisions, loose with cash'. In fact, the link between old age and poverty was so firm that many ancients would have agreed immediately with Yeats' lines,

> An aged man is but a paltry thing,
> A tattered coat upon a stick . . .

In *The Madness of Heracles* Euripides has his ageing chorus sing

> Ah, youth is kind; but age is always a weight
> heavier than the rocks of Etna
> bearing down on my head,
> covering my eyes
> with a dark cloak.
> Please, I wouldn't take the wealth
> of an Asian tyrant,
> nor halls full of gold
> in exchange for youth,
> the most beautiful thing in times of wealth,
> the most beautiful thing in times of poverty. [14]

Cicero has that passage in mind, not only when he makes Scipio say that old men go about as though they are bearing the burden of Mount Etna, but also, I think, when Cato says that old age can be difficult in times of affluence and poverty alike. In doing so, he takes the chorus's attitude head on, and suggests that old age, too, can have its blessings, even if someone elderly is poor. But the passage from *The Madness of Heracles* is stuck in some deeply Greek thinking about the nature of beauty itself. Their word for beautiful – *kalos* – was so bound up with notions of goodness and nobility that Euripides goes so far as to suggest that youth, too, is akin to elevated status and even a high moral worth. In short, youth is its own wealth, its own classiness; *jeunesse* itself really is *dorée*.

As Parkin points out, anthropologists studying African societies have identified 'age-class' systems in which the elderly gain rather than lose power. However much the ancients tried to articulate the values of respect for the elderly, and aimed to give them not only prestige but also power, the rhetoric of money and a more fiscal sort of value seems to undermine that hierarchy. It could be that youth becomes associated with metaphorical money just as old age retains its links with actual cash, but the appearance of an old man sans absolutely every-thing feels more pathetic than shocking. This makes the old Oedipus a stronger representative of old age than Cato:

> Who'll welcome wandering Oedipus today
> with offerings that are barely adequate?
> I'm only after little, and I get
> less than a little; still, it sorts me out.[15]

We might expect Oedipus' begging to be an embarrass-ment to his family – can't they look after him? – but his daughter Antigone is doing her best under the circumstances. Given his troubled past, no town wants Oedipus to stay in it too long.[16] Here he looks and sounds like a *schnorrer*, which needn't be a bad thing: in Yiddish, that term, meaning 'beggar', isn't always an insult, because it is a good deed or a blessing (*mitzvah*) to have someone in the community to whom you can show compassion (*rakhmones*). It's for this reason that Homer regrets that his hero has lost the opportunity to look after his parents. It's worth bearing the idea in mind, along with other Homeric lines, spoken by Eumaeus the swineherd:

> Stranger, insulting strangers isn't right,
> even when they're in greater need than you –
> each stranger and each beggar comes from God.

This is what makes Ovid's account of Baucis and Philemon all the more moving. In his *Metamorphoses* he tells the story of how Zeus and Hermes came down from Mount Olympus to see if humans were generous enough to give them shelter. Nobody is, except for an elderly couple in a remote cottage. The meagreness of their offerings is feelingly evoked. The gods reward Baucis and Philemon by allowing them to die at the same time, and the pair turn into conjoined trees. Again, Ovid appears to subvert the cliché: the old might be poor, but they're not misers. As we learn from St Mark's Gospel, the reverse is as likely, if not more so:

And Jesus sat over against the treasury, and beheld how the people cast money into the treasury: and many that were rich cast in much. And there came a certain poor widow, and she threw in two mites, which make a farthing. And he called unto him his disciples, and saith unto them, Verily I say unto you, That this poor widow hath cast more in, than all they which have cast into the treasury: For all they did cast in of their abundance; but she of her want did cast in all that she had, even all her living.[17]

Can we take anything from this?

The pressing need to take better care of an ever-growing elderly population is what makes us look most urgently at other cultures. It's why Jeremy Hunt looked towards Japan, China and India; it's why I'm looking at the ancient world. Mary Beard delivered a piece on Radio 4's *A Point of View*, in which she started from the myth of Tithonus.[18] In this myth the goddess of dawn, Eos, fell in love with a young mortal and asked that he could live for ever. Her mistake was that she didn't ask if he could stay young for ever; and Beard uses the image of Tithonus babbling behind shiny doors, which is picking up on her rendering of the Homeric Hymn as a way to convey how dependent we can become. It also reminds us of how ignored the elderly can be: 'When most of us get to the frail stage we're past speaking out, as that long non-death of Tithonus reminds us.'

Beard goes on to talk compassionately about the circumstances in which carers work and the pittance for which they're expected to do it. She draws a comparison between the difficulties of looking after the elderly and looking after children, and even though the ancients, from Pythagoras onwards, look at old age as a second childhood, Beard reminds us that the link can be insulting.

Beard doesn't directly ask for more money; de Hennezel comes closer with a classy, mordant line on euthanasia: 'One thing is certain: it would be a lot cheaper to pass a law enabling doctors to kill all the old people who are threatening suicide because they can no longer bear being ill-treated, than to free up the money needed to increase the quality of careers in caring for the very elderly and thereby enable elderly people to be treated properly.'[19]

And then there's Jeremy Hunt, talking to an audience of carers and social workers as he looks to the East. Look at the debate from a distance, and it goes down classic left–right lines: between the welfare state and the Big Society; between paying carers more and doing it yourself. Again, though, both sides are castigating us for being so reluctant to care for the elderly. And they're both right.

So what are our excuses? They're not so bad either, particularly if we're members of the sandwich generation, worrying about parents and children simultaneously. It's here that the real business of *threpteria* happens: parents can be nurses to their children and also sometimes to their parents.

It makes time hard to manage, and leads to stress and lose–lose choices.

In Japan, the problem is more acute because the elderly are already significantly more numerous than the generation following them. But Japan has a tradition of volunteering – a society that's already big – and a government that's good at fostering volunteer work. It also has a range of credit systems, or means of bartering. To this end, since 1995 some have experimented with a system called *fureai kippu* – 'caring relationship tickets' – so that someone who helps an elderly person by doing the shopping, say, or housework, can earn credits which they can in theory use when they are older, or else exchange for care of their own family. The scheme is heartening, but it's too soon to see if it is working since, if the elderly need this kind of service, they are less likely to be able to return it in kind.

The Japanese model could be telling us that the Big Society can work as long as it has some kind of intervention, or nannying, from some overarching organisation. It could be telling us that desperate times need bold and original ideas. But, as we look back on classical times and the obligation to offer *threpteria*, we see that relationships between the old and the young are too complicated, and sometimes too bitter, to be left solely to the human instinct for love and filial devotion, or even shame. As Parkin's discussion of birth rates in traditional societies suggests, we are only likely to have a cohesive way of caring for the elderly if there's something in it for the generation doing the caring.

6

The old in public life

Nestor loved talking. He was the elder statesman of the Greeks, and talked out his days behind the lines at the Trojan War. He would talk about how much it was worth listening to him. He would talk about how he talked. He would talk extensively about the past. He was Agamemnon's chief adviser during the Trojan War, and as Cicero says, 'The Greek leader never wishes he had ten men like Ajax, but like Nestor instead, and he had no doubt that if that had been his lot then Troy would have collapsed rapidly.' Make that fairly rapidly: if you take any speech of Nestor's and multiply it by ten and then allow time for some disagreement, you may think that by the end of the conflict the warriors would have been old men themselves.

There are times when Nestor seems to be a parody of an old man, and his advice can sometimes have disastrous consequences. A troubling example is the way he sends Patroclus into battle and ultimately to his death. It's certainly a tragedy, but it has the effect of bringing Achilles into the war.

One reading suggests that Nestor was valuable because he was playing a long game. He was no prophet – for example, he didn't spot that a dream Agamemnon had was a false one sent by Zeus – but he had seen enough of life and action to have a view of how things turned out. And so he was taken seriously.

Plutarch wrote a whole treatise on the subject of elder statesmen called *Should the Elderly Run the Country?* Yes, was his answer. Whereas young men bring the gifts of their bodies to the state, the old bring the gifts of the soul, the *psyche*, which Plutarch lists as justice, moderation and wisdom. Moderation is crucial. The stinginess that Aristotle finds so bothersome in the elderly, and the instinct to equivocate rather than assert, becomes to others a valuable resource. As Plutarch writes, 'Pericles' administration gained its greatest power when he was old, which was when he persuaded the Athenians to engage in the war; and when they were eager to fight at an unfavourable time against 60,000 heavily armed men, he intervened and prevented it.'

An extreme example of reverence for old age in politics comes from the third-century Roman senate, who chose a septuagenarian called Tacitus to be emperor. When he tried to decline, citing his years, the senators called out, 'Trajan was an old man when he came to power,' ten times, and then said the same about Hadrian ten times. From Tacitus they thought they would be safe from immaturity, excessive haste or fearful roughness.[1] Cicero has Cato assert a simple rule: young people overthrow states, and the old put them back together. In his account of old age in ancient Greece Robert Garland puts the same thing more negatively: 'As in the modern world, so in antiquity, gerontocracies are not noted for radical solutions, while societies which undergo rapid changes tend to manifest little respect for the elderly.'[2]

For Cicero's Cato, this is a distinction between Sparta and Athens:

> For example, it's on record that when a mature man arrived in the theatre during the Athenian festival, none of his own fellow citizens in the large crowd gave up their place for him, but when he came to the Spartan seats (they had set seating because they were diplomats), it's said that they all rose for him and reserved a seat for the old man. Upon this, when there was repeated applause from the whole crowd, one of the Spartans said that Athenians know what's right, but they don't want to do it.[3]

Certainly Sparta made its respect for the elderly clearer in its constitution. The highest body in the kingdom of Sparta was the *gerousia*. Its enormous powers − to propose their own motions, to veto those proposed by others, to interpret the law, to try murder cases − were in the hands of 30 men. Two of these were the hereditary Spartan kings, and the rest all had to be older than 60. The Areopagus, for a while the supreme judicial and legislative body in Athens, was a council of elders. In Ovid's *Fasti*, in which the poet looks for the origins of Roman traditions, he even sees the authority of the elderly in the calendar:

> Once, whitening heads were held in great respect,
> and wrinkles given the due that is correct.
> Youths did the work of Mars − fought savage wars,
> holding their places for a holy cause.
> The weaker age group, being less use in war,
> would take the role of national counsellor;
> only the old could pass the council's door −

its name was 'senate', since it was mature.
The old gave people laws – rulings would gauge
what rank you could aspire to at what age.
When old men walked with young, they'd not
    offend –
they'd go on the inside when they took a friend.
Who'd risk an utterance that would bring a blush
in front of the old? Old age would make them hush.
Romulus saw this, and made certain souls
Fathers – he gave to them the state's controls.
I sense these majors gave their name to May,
and ruled to make things go old age's way.
Numitor might have said, 'Give to the old
a month.' His grandson did as he was told.
The next month's name suggests this is the truth:
June, as in 'juniors', is the month of youth.[4]

Ovid here plays with the natural link between the words
'senate' and 'senior' and adds a new, more tenuous verbal
proof that language itself demonstrates the natural authority
that the elderly should have. But the poet retains his awareness that this view is nostalgic with his fond mention of a
custom that makes a young man walk on the outer side of
the pavement if he's accompanying an older one.[5] And this
passage, which Ovid puts into the mouth of Urania, the
muse of astronomy, has its less reverential moments, such
as the hint that the elderly are likely to run the state in
their own interests: if old people have a reputation for being
tight, this puts the problem onto the national stage.

Although the name 'senate' supposes that its members
would more likely be senior, in practice it didn't work out
that way: the senate of the empire had a minimum age of

25, and after a certain age (sometimes 60, sometimes 65) a senator was no longer obliged to attend meetings.[6] This suggests there was a notional retirement age and that after a certain time a senator's gifts of the soul were no longer indispensable. Certainly there were limits to physically active life – a Roman soldier need no longer be on active service after the age of 46. But the idea of a retirement age is an odd one. (We've already seen how murky it is when looking at slaves, with Cato saying that you should sell old ones, and Pliny having to find work for senior slaves if he's not to carry out their long-deferred execution.) The unified Germany was the first country to introduce a retirement age, in 1889, and it was set at 70. The idea was that national security would provide for 'those who are disabled from work by age and invalidity', and to reach 70 in 1889 was less likely than it is now. Jeremy Hunt's world is clearly different from Otto von Bismarck's: 'And the cruel irony of the pockets of failure that let the whole system down is that old age can be wonderful. Freed from the responsibility of work – and having cast off some of the stresses and preoccupations that can dominate earlier years – many older people thrive like never before, even as they battle infirmity.'

Seventy was a key age in Rome too. Roman men were required to offer their services to the state, either by making financial contributions or else by giving up to five days a year, working on such things as maintaining roads or buildings; citizens were exempt from these duties – *munera* – before they were 25 and after they were 70.[7] So 70 provides a useful definition of old age, or at least, physical old age, but when we're considering the age at which a person can contribute to the running of a state as a counsellor or legislator, the process of ageing and withdrawing from service to the state becomes a more fluid one in the ancient world. Like with medicine, it depended on an individual knowing his own limits. Seneca was in favour of retirement and withdrawal from public life, and in a letter discusses a friend of his addressee who should ignore the jibes of those who say he's abandoning his career.[8] Pliny the Younger, too, likes the idea of a quiet life, and hopes that his last years can be his own, but, as with the friend of Seneca's friend, he worries that he may be thought to be seeking not peace but indolence.

Although Plutarch spends a while advancing the opposite view, he does so compassionately: 'A man's eagerness shouldn't fail before his strength, but when it is deserted by strength, it shouldn't be forced.' Both Plutarch and Cicero acknowledged that some duties were hard or impossible for some because of their age; Plutarch concluded that duties should be given to individuals according to their abilities, and in *On Old Age* we read, 'It is right that you should use what strength you have, and do whatever your strength allows you to do.' In the ideal state he proposes in his *Laws* Plato has a plan that is an ideal compromise: the elderly should sing in a chorus to Dionysus, and because they might be more inhibited about performing, they should be given wine to help them.[9] Athens reserved certain roles for women past childbearing age, such as midwifery and mourning.

The length of a public life is a difficult thing to gauge, as debates about the retirement age keep reminding us. Any phone-in on the subject will have as many contributors saying they want to keep active as there will be others who don't want to be worked into the ground. Kenneth Clarke put the latter position neatly when he stepped down from the cabinet: 'I've just celebrated another birthday, so I thought I was about to retire. I was expecting to retire at the last reshuffle, but I stayed on . . . If you do work beyond the normal retirement age, I think actually you should be prepared to decide you're going to go, rather than waiting for people to scratch their heads and think of reasons for getting rid of you.'[10]

Which leads to the deeper question of when the elderly stop being, or at least stop feeling, useful to society. In the ancient world a culture of respect prevailed. Yes, this was honoured occasionally in the breach rather than the observance, and more honoured in the breach if you read a writer such as Aristophanes, who gives the chorus in *Knights* a list to recite of the once popular writers nobody takes seriously now they're old. And yet that tradition of respect was impossible to ignore. As a result, the elderly could at least assert their right to be heard, so that those around them could draw on their experience and reflections. They were role models, and the relationship between the old and the young was thought to be mutually beneficial. 'What is more pleasant,' asks Cicero, 'than old age surrounded by the zeal of youth?' He has Cato suggest to his younger listeners that his company is pleasant for them too.

There's the charming image of Plutarch that he himself provides in *Should the Elderly Run the Country*: 'Now you know that I have been serving the Pythian Apollo for many Pythiads, but you wouldn't say, "Plutarch, you've done enough sacrificing, marching in processions, and dancing in choruses, and now that you're older it is time to put off the garland and to desert the oracle because of your age."' Did Plutarch have a strong sense of duty? Or was it that his duties were particularly compelling? It's a two-way process between the state continuing to value the contributions that the elderly make to it, and the elderly being willing to make those contributions which depends on the nature of the state itself. A state that engages its citizens is going to retain their involvement for longer. Athens provides a useful demonstration. There was a body of 6,000 men, all over the age of 30, who were allowed to serve on juries. (Juries in Athens were large – 201 men would hear private cases, with 501 for cases of state importance.) Jurors would receive three obols a day, which wasn't a living, but at least it was pocket money; as a result the rich need not apply, and a day at the law court became a rewarding pastime for the elderly. The comic playwright Aristophanes, who was antipathetic towards so many of the people having so much of the power, found the set-up ridiculous, and made fun of it in his play *The Wasps*. He had the perfect butt for his joke: somebody old and poor, eating lentil soup and demanding his three obols. Even from Aristophanes' partial viewpoint, the play dramatises the relationship between the elderly and the state. To him it looked populist to hand justice over to cash-poor time-rich freeloaders; to many audiences now, it mightn't look so bad.

Plutarch has one more piece of advice about the elderly who are thinking of playing a part in politics. It'll be familiar by now: start early. There's no point, he says, in doing something completely different for most of your career and then deciding to have a pop at government. This follows the logic of Cicero's fundamental principle throughout *On Old Age* – if you're not having a good old age, the fault isn't in old age, but in you.

Can we take anything from this?

In 2014 the UK government announced that it would ask people between the ages of 70 and 75 to serve on juries. This is surely good news, although it raises the question: why stop at 75? The model Aristophanes knocks is surely not such a bad one: people with experience, wisdom and the time to devote to the community are perfectly qualified to judge their peers (or more likely their juniors), especially if the whole point of their role is to bring good sense to the question rather than legal expertise. It doesn't fall foul of Plutarch's rule, either – that we shouldn't take up a new career with no preparation for it. It's a reminder of the put-down Margaret Atwood used on a brain surgeon who mused that he would take up writing on retirement. 'What a coincidence,' she replied, 'because when I retire, I'm going to be a brain surgeon.'[11] And Proust has a simile involving a distinguished artist who can take any amount of criticism about his paintings but becomes touchy if you joke about his new hobbies, such as cookery or gardening.

So, if an old person wants to contribute to public life, Plutarch says, start early, but the jury system allows an opening, as does the magistracy or even local councils; and if he or she doesn't want to contribute, then, in the tradition of starting early, it's better to say, 'I'm going to devote more time to . . .' than 'I'm going to take up . . .'

7

The old mind

It's harsh to hear Cicero blame the unhappy old person for his or her unhappiness, even if he does concede that poverty can contrive to make happiness all the more remote. We are so much more aware of specific mental illnesses than the ancients, but even in our own society many fail to acknowledge that depression or addiction are diseases. It's true that those ancients who called the young hot-tempered, and the old cold, were working from assumptions that their own principles of medicine had established. But Aristotle, among others, was applying those assumptions generally: he was trying to establish scientific laws. In his view the fault really was with old age. It took a more hands-on day-to-day physician such as Galen to see patients as individuals with distinct needs. Even so, he didn't blame the elderly for their difficulties, which came from attacks on their bodies and minds.

And so it was easy to take the general view that the elderly were forgetful. We'd be going too far to say that an old man in court was assumed to be of unsound mind until proven *compos mentis*, but every allowance was made for the possibility that they didn't know what was going on. Solon's laws on wills included the stipulation that those making them should be of sound mind 'because testaments extorted through the frenzy of a disease, or dotage of old age, were not in fact the wills of the people who made them'. And, as we have seen, he also allowed that a will could include an heir from outside the family, provided judgement was not impaired by pain, violence, drugs, old age, or 'the influence of a woman'. But demonstrating unimpaired judgement took some doing, if an often-told story about Sophocles is a guide. Cicero and Plutarch both tell of how the dramatist's children challenged his will because at 90 he was unlikely to have meant what he'd written. In his defence, he recited a chorus from the play he was writing, *Oedipus at Colonus*. The jurors are said to have vindicated him and carried him out of the court with loud cheers.

The generalisation that a form of dementia comes as if inevitably with old age goes back as far as Pythagoras, who thought that in the last stages of life 'the system returns to the imbecility of infancy's first stage'. The writings of the Hippocratic corpus agreed that mental disabilities were normal – illnesses, yes, but normal. Aristotle's blanket prognosis is just as bleak: 'There is not much left of the acumen of the mind which helped them in their youth, nor of the faculties which served the intellect, and which some call judgement, imagination, power of reasoning and memory. They see them gradually blunted by deterioration and see that they can hardly fulfil their function.'

Galen started from quite a different perspective. For one thing, he took the view that the brain was the seat of thought, rather than the heart, as Aristotle insisted – Aristotle argued that the brain was for keeping the heart cool. Galen thought of increasing mental failure as a disease rather than a likely aspect of old age, and to him it was a disease that attacked individuals. As a result, he questioned whether it was peculiar to old people, although he thought that problems arising from old age could bring it on. The disease he called *morosis* could completely obliterate knowledge of letters and other skills, and sufferers were unable to remember their own names. It's one of the few subjects that makes Juvenal say anything compassionate about anyone ever:

> Dementia's worse than all physical loss –
> forgetting slaves' names, or the face of a friend
> who came last night to supper, or the children
> one parented and reared.[1]

Jonathan Swift uses this idea when anticipating his own decline:

> Besides, his memory decays,
> He recollects not what he says;
> He cannot call his friends to mind;
> Forgets the place where last he dined . . .[2]

Cicero remarks on it too: 'But then, there's the fading memory . . . [And yet] the elderly remember everything they care about: the dates of court hearings; to whom they owe money; who owes it to them.'[3] Commenting on these ancient observations, two researchers in the field of memory and dementia, N. C. Berchtold and C. W. Cotman, conclude that 'the Greco-Roman diagnosis of senile debility undoubtedly included dementia due to a number of causes, including central nervous system infections, depression, vitamin deficiency, cerebral infarcts, among others . . .'[4] For them, Cicero is unusually progressive, and it's true that, seen from the perspective of mental health, Cicero is rare in urging us to approach mental infirmity in the same way as we would physical:

> And really it's not just the body that needs support – the mind and the spirit require even more; because old age extinguishes these, too, if you don't add oil to the lamp. And while bodies slump with the fatigue of exercise, exercise lifts the spirits. When Statius calls old men 'stupid comic actors', he means the credulous, the forgetful, the careless – these are not the faults of old age, but of an inactive, lazy, drowsy old age . . . the stupidity of the old, which is often called delirium, is characteristic not of all old people, but just the silly ones.[5]

This is where Cicero offers some guidance worth taking seriously today. He has Cato mention the Greek statesman Themistocles, who claimed to know the names of every Athenian citizen – it's often estimated that there were 20,000 of them – and Cato speaks of his own useful habit: each evening he recalls to himself everything that he's said or done that day. It's a practice that brings Tony Benn to mind, who would end each day by recording his thoughts in diary form to a Dictaphone; and it's good to think that Cicero did something similar. Cicero quotes approvingly a saying of Solon – 'I grow old learning something new every day' – and says, 'These are the exercises of the intellect and the racetracks of the mind. By sweating through these workouts, I don't much miss my physical strength.'

There was plenty of evidence that those who kept their

minds active throughout their lives were still as sharp in their old age, if not sharper: Plutarch remarks in his treatise on elder statesmen that there is no one whose youth isn't surpassed by his mature years. Sophocles wasn't an isolated case: Euripides died in his seventies, and two highly original plays, *Iphigenia at Aulis* and *The Bacchae*, were produced posthumously. As Cicero reports, Plato was still at work at the end of his life, and so on.

But is it possible that these uplifting examples fought off the difficulties and diseases of old age by willpower alone? Probably not. Nowadays we would say they were lucky not to have been afflicted by Alzheimer's, but we also continue to believe that we can stave off encroaching mental infirmity by exercising our brains. The excellent U3A – the University of the Third Age – is a tribute to this, and friends of mine have been telling me of their parents' activities, such as crosswords, sudoku or language learning. Among the many things that researchers advance as ways to reduce or combat the effects of Alzheimer's is speaking a second language.★ Actually, this research points towards the regular use of a second language in someone who is bilingual, so that the brain is constantly encountering equivalent words or concepts between two languages. If this is so, then the ancient Romans in particular were at an advantage: Rome was a bilingual culture, and all educated Romans knew the Greek language and literature intimately.

Moses Finley, writing in 1981, speculated that the elderly of the ancient world had to be physiologically and psychologically tough to have reached old age, and that this in itself helped to account for a possibly higher rate of intellectual

---

★ See, for example, the *New York Times* interview with the researcher Ellen Bialystock (May 30, 2011).

achievement among the ancients than we observe in our own society. At least, as he puts it, 'My impression is that the Verdis, Picassos and Bertrand Russells of (at least Greek) antiquity constituted a larger proportion of that class of men than their modern counterparts.' This is an alarming sentence for many reasons – not least because it's exactly like Cicero's argument that a kind of innate rigour may well see you through. (There's nothing wrong in agreeing with Cicero – it's just that Finley writes off *On Old Age* as a non-starter.) More alarming still is the idea that someone as wise as Finley was perhaps already susceptible to the modern media's promotion of youth over age in its pursuit of the hottest new thing – the debut novelist, the Young British Artist, the Next Generation poet. The idea that a young artist can trump an older one is a strongly Romantic one – that early Wordsworth is better than late, or that Keats is better than either, or that Mozart is better than Salieri.

It's true, as writers about old age assert, that the elderly were marginalised. This did happen to artists, as a chorus by a youthful Aristophanes reminds us. In his play *Knights* he mocks the audience for no longer remembering the comic playwrights of the past:

> He [Cratinus] flourished.
> But now when you see him talking drivel, you don't
>   pity him
> as his electron lyre pegs fall out, its tone gone,
> its strings yawning. But he's an old man, running
>   around
> like Connas, with a dry crown, and ruined by drink –
> given his former triumphs, he ought to be drinking
>   in the Prytaneion![6]

This passage suggests mental as well as physical failing, along with the depressive impact of lost fame. While dementia was clearly present in the ancient world, it was less noticeable than it is now, given the relative scarcity of significantly old people. But they thought about it, and their thinking about the end of life, and the prospects of other illness, is something we can try applying to our own experiences of mental and physical incapacity in old age, especially where it elides with our own debates about euthanasia and the ethics of assisted dying.

As we have seen, the ancients were not reliably sympathetic in their views on mental infirmity. Cicero argues, 'To those who look within themselves for all good things, nothing that the necessity of nature brings can seem bad.' Right from the start of *On Old Age*, he's asserting his philosophical position: he is sympathetic to the doctrines of Stoicism.

The Stoics, who began teaching in Athens in the late fourth century BC, developed a philosophical system that embraced logic – or at least, they embraced the idea that nature itself is logical and that the universe has its own 'logos'. To think logically is to think in harmony with nature, and nature is always reasonable. When we say now that somebody is taking an illness stoically, we tend to mean they're being brave. The word 'stoical' has come to mean that because of the fuller sense that a Stoic accepted the principles of nature. The idea is so germane to Cicero's language of 'necessity' and 'nature' that it begins to affect his imagery: an unripe apple will resist if we try plucking it from the tree, whereas a mature one will simply fall. To resist is to fail to accept. And failing to accept is your fault. Worse, it takes you from the path of virtue – the ultimate good (*summum bonum*) that is the goal, the end, of life. The founder of the school, Zeno, is a characterful example of the Stoic at his most attentive to the reason of the universe. Diogenes Laertius tells us that Zeno broke his toe as he was leaving his students, cried out, 'I'm coming, I'm coming, why are you calling for me?' and held his breath until he died. He was approximately 72 years old.

Cicero takes a moment to attack those who oppose this view of the world. The followers of Epicurus didn't see virtue as something worth pursuing for its own sake. How decadent that must have sounded to the Roman ear, just as people today think of 'epicurean' as a synonym of 'gourmet'. But the arguments of the Epicureans aren't really like that. What Epicurus actually wanted us to do was not to pursue pleasure, but rather to avoid discomfort, pain, anxiety. When Epicurus said, 'The stomach is the measure of all things,' he wasn't really talking about how great food is. It's more important to take from this the idea that you should use your stomach to know when you've had too much. In the long term, to stuff yourself is going to make you uncomfortable, no matter how pleasurable the stuffing was.

All of which chimes with what we're learning about old age. Know yourself. Know your limits. If the desire is there but the strength isn't, let it go, as Plutarch suggests. At odd moments we find Cicero stumbling into this line of thought himself. After his mention of Sophocles' remark about feeling free of a raging master when no longer longing for sex, Cicero says, 'The lack of such things is perhaps unpleasant and annoying to someone who wants them, but to someone who's sated and glutted with them, it's better to lack them than to enjoy them.' Here Cicero appeals to the sense of moderation he finds in the elderly. And there's a sense – a fairly depressing one – that this notion of the elderly being more likely to live moderate lives comes from the idea that they want less pleasure, or at least that they expect less of it: as Cicero says, old age is the time for eking out (*demetendis*) the fruit that we've gathered, and for appreciating it (*percipiendis*). The suggestion is that we pace our pleasures, to make them last through our declining years.

These are ideas we can apply to many of the things we have considered throughout this discussion. Not too much food. Not too much exercise. If physical work is too much, attempt mental strife instead. Keep your humours as much in balance as possible. While other ancients frown on make-up and accessories, Ovid encourages them. But not too much. Marie de Hennezel's chapter 'A sensual old age' might lead us to apply some of these ideas to sex too. In it she listens to the elderly whose intimacy is enhanced rather than impeded by a lack of orgasm. As Cicero sensitively puts it, although he's not talking about sex, 'Although old age doesn't have such a range of pleasures available to it, it doesn't altogether lack them.' He likens the difference between youth and old age to watching a comic actor from the front row and the back: 'Youth is perhaps happier looking at pleasures close up, but looking at them from further away is cheering enough.' Put this way, it can sound like a limiting of expectations – Cicero doesn't take the next step and say, 'And the view's better from the back, not to mention the acoustics' – but throughout his treatise he does at least imply that to be no longer distracted by desires is its own joy. Seneca puts it directly: 'I consider that old age, reaching the last finishing post, has its own pleasures; or else, this one thing follows in place of pleasure: to need nothing. How pleasant it is to have exhausted desires, and to have left them.'

This idea explains why Cicero has no patience with people who complain about old age. And, as we've seen, the ancient world was full of writers who delighted in satirising the elderly for their gloomy outlooks – their love of talking about the past, their haste to chide the young and their urgent need to cling to a life about which they keep moaning. And yet we can't really blame them, if there's an assumption that even the pleasures we have will become less pleasurable.

It's death that puts this into perspective, and death which, according to many of the ancients, makes us cherish even the life that has the least pleasure to offer. We have already heard Admetus snarl that sentiment accusingly at his father when the old man wouldn't die in his place.[7] The poet Anacreon puts this at its most bittersweet:

> The women say, 'You're old,
> Anacreon; pick up
> a mirror and you'll see
> your hair's no longer there;
> your forehead's bald as well.'
> Whether it's there or not
> I don't know. This I know:
> it's right that an old man
> should have more fun when fate
> is coming close to him.

We even have to fear that we'll fear death itself, which brings us to the question about old age that has come to dominate our ethical debates: what can we do when life has nothing left to offer? When we have lost not only our pleasures, but also our health and even our minds?

As with the debates about sex, our views on the subject of euthanasia, or suicide, or assisted suicide, are different in a post-Christian society. The idea that life has sanctity depends on the understanding that it is a divine gift. As the columnist Sam Leith wrote in a piece defending the right to die, 'We hold life valuable not because it is on loan from God, or because it is an abstract societal good, but by virtue of each individual life being the absolute possession of the person living it.'[8] Once we look at the problem freed from the lenses of the Abrahamic religions, we can engage with the debate as the ancients did.

They had their own concerns about suicide. After all, our most instinctive response is likely to be an ancient one: what about the Hippocratic oath? It's a fair point, because the followers of Hippocrates swore that they would do no harm to their patients, so assisting a suicide was out of the question. But, as today, suicide, of a kind, was not out of the question. Whereas today a doctor may live with her or his conscience by withdrawing treatment rather than by taking active steps to end life, in classical times the simplest compromise an old person could reach was to stop eating.

There was a debate because people disagreed, and the disagreements didn't just depend on which school of philosophy one preferred. It's worth asking the question: who would oppose suicide more, the Epicurean or the Stoic? It is easy to assume that the Epicurean, with his emphasis on comfort, would seek to avoid pain, and to abandon it at last, whereas the Stoic would accept it as part of his destiny. But actually they don't respond like that.

In his ingenious book *Facing Death: Epicurus and His Critics* (2004) James Warren comes up with a sequence of answers to the question: what did the people who avoided worry do when there was only one thing left to worry about? One consolation about the inevitability of death has been put pithily in Latin: *non fui, fui, non sum, non curo* ('I didn't exist, I did exist, I don't exist, I don't care'). Even Cicero found something reassuring about this: 'If I don't feel anything when I'm dead, as some small-time philosophers believe, then I don't worry that those dead philosophers may be chuckling at my mistake.'

But their apparent insouciance about death didn't mean that they embraced it. After all, that wouldn't make sense. If you're so afraid of death that it makes your life not worth living, then all suicide does is demonstrate that you have given in to that fear, as if you had learned nothing from Epicurus and his teachings. Warren quotes the poet Lucretius, whose poetry did much to preserve the tenets of Epicureanism:

> Often, by fearing death, hatred of life,
> of seeing light, depresses people so
> that they connive with death, grieving at heart,
> forgetting that this fear's their fount of cares.[9]

And yet, death *would* stop that worry. What can an Epicurean do? Warren leaves the question open: 'The position has reached something of a stalemate since, of course, the Epicurean living the good life will not, it is expected, have any reason to commit suicide . . . the default assumption, as it were, is that one will continue to live unless and until such a time when life becomes too painful even for the Epicurean wise man. After all, until such a time the Epicurean's life is a pleasant and happy one.'*

The Stoic, who does not see himself or herself as living for pleasure, takes a different view. There is nothing to be

---

* James Warren, *Facing Death: Epicurus and his Critics* (Oxford, 2004), 209.

gained from this clinging to life. Seneca the Younger's letters to his younger correspondent, a procurator of Sicily called Lucilius, rehearse the Stoic position compellingly, and his letter on the body, the soul and suicide is worth quoting extensively. He begins with a discussion of Platonic forms. Like Socrates in Plato's account of the philosopher's death, the *Phaedo*,[10] Seneca asserts that the matter of the world is unstable, whereas what we can't see is eternal:

Plato does not include the things we see or touch among those things that he considers 'to be' by his definition; they are fluid, and are in a constant state of waxing and waning. None of us is the same in old age as he was in his youth; none of us is the same in the morning as he was the day before. Our bodies are taken along like rivers are. Anything you see runs with time; nothing of the things we see remains; even while I'm saying those things are changed, I am changed. This is what Heraclitus says: 'We step into the same river twice, and don't step into it.' The name of the river is the same, and the water is dispersed.

This is more noticeable in a river than in a person; but no less swift a current transports us, too, and consequently I'm amazed at our madness, because we love so dearly something so fleeting as the body, and we fear that some time we will die, when every moment there is a death of our previous self. Do you want to fear something happening once, when it happens every day? I have been talking about the human being, whose substance is in flux, is decayed and damaged by all factors; but the world, too, that eternal, unbeaten thing, is changed – it doesn't stay the same. Although it has in itself everything it had before, it has it in a different way – it changes its order. [11]

Like Cicero at the end of his *On Old Age*, Seneca finds reassurance in the idea that a higher sphere awaits us. As we have already seen, Cicero allows that this might be a mistake, but that his life is better for having been lived under this delusion. In this way he is like Blaise Pascal, who argued that if life is a wager, then it's better to bet on God, since the consequences are happier. Faith may remain a comfort for some, but not for others; and for many the notion that the world itself ends, or that the laws of thermodynamics anticipate that our universe will undergo a 'heat death', is equally depressing. If, as Seneca says elsewhere, he will remain alive to those who survive him, then the prospect of none of our descendants, however remote, prolonging any fraction of our legacy, is a gloomy one.[12] And so, like Plato and Cicero, he seeks an imperishable world beyond this one and beyond our senses.

Even the process of seeking that world reassures Seneca in the face of inevitable death. In one letter he picks up his refrain that philosophy itself is a comfort and worth studying as much for the practical benefits it brings as for the pleasure it affords.[13] He takes Plato's long life and his hardiness as a way to make not only philosophy, but also philosophers, useful to his reader; we are again reminded of Cicero's thesis that a healthy long life is dependent on a restrained attitude towards pleasures. 'Frugality,' Seneca says, 'can lead to old age, which I don't think is worth desiring, nor spurning; pleasure in one's own company can last the longest time, when people have made their own company worth enjoying.'

After this, Seneca's letter heads off in a surprising direction. He justifies suicide. If it seems an odd moment in his treatise to do that, then perhaps we should think again about

Socrates, who when given the chance to escape his execution argues that he would rather go through with it. Having established that the body is mortal, he sees that there are reasons why, under certain circumstances, the soul may be freed from it.

So we will come to a conclusion about whether it is right to loathe the extremes of old age and, rather than waiting for the end, to bring it about by one's own hand. Whoever idly awaits his fate, like the wine lover who drinks the amphora dry and soaks up the dregs as well, is close to being a coward. But we need to ask whether the climax of life is dregs or the clearest, most liquid part – meaning that the mind is unharmed and functioning senses support the spirit, and the body isn't deficient, or moribund. This affects whether someone is extending a life, or a death.

But if the body is unable to function, why wouldn't it be right to let the struggling soul go? And perhaps that is worth doing a little earlier than it is due, in case you can't do it when you should; and when there's a greater risk of living badly than of dying quickly, only a fool would trade the possibility of something great against the trade-off of a little more time. Old age leads few people towards their deaths without some impairment, and an inactive, unuseful life has awaited many.

So do you think that to have lost some life is any crueller than the law against ending it? Don't hear me out unsympathetically, as if my talking thinking applied directly to you, and consider what I'm saying: I will not leave old age, if it leaves me with the whole of myself – the whole of my better part; but if old age were to start jangling my mind, if it tears the mind to pieces, and if it leaves me not with a life but with the soul alone, I would flee that tumbling, decaying house. I will not escape disease by death, as long as the disease is treatable, and not an imposition on my mental faculties. I will not take my life by my own hands because of pain – that way, to die is to be defeated. But if I learn that this pain is something I have to suffer for the rest of my life, I will leave, not because of the pain itself, but because it would obstruct everything that makes my life worth living. It is weak and cowardly to die because of the pain, but stupid to live for pain's sake.

But I am going on too long, and the day can be given to other things. And how can someone end a life, if he can't end a letter?[14]

This is a dramatic and disturbing glimpse of old age, and Seneca confronts not only his own fears but those we have encountered throughout this look at the elderly in antiquity: a fear of physical and mental decay. Today it can read as a compelling case against the prosecution of those who assist a suicide: 'in case you can't do it when you should'. That *should* is the mark of the Stoic, who wants to know what right path is ordained for him or her. It should be said that Seneca did take his own life, in a hot bath – not because he was ill, but because he was implicated in a plot to kill his former pupil, the emperor Nero.

Seneca would urge his students not to take philosophy out of context, and this sentiment about facing and embracing death in old age needs balancing with his other thoughts. If the letter above makes it look as though Seneca would have made the journey to Dignitas, it appears less likely from a later one. He was a Stoic in the more popular sense of putting up with adversity gallantly, as well as in the sense of learning and following his own *logos*, or reason, or fate. He lists the heartening thoughts that have brought him through his afflictions. He includes the cajolings, the vigils and the prayers of his friends, and would appear to agree with Jeremy Hunt that 'loneliness is as bad for one's health as smoking fifteen cigarettes a day'. Unsurprisingly, Seneca also finds a remedy in the joy of philosophy itself.

It is sad for me that you are taxed by repeated bouts of catarrh and by the brief fevers that are apt to follow the long catarrhs, because I too have experienced this kind of illness, which I dismissed at first; in adolescence, it was possible to bear injuries and to wage war against disease aggressively. Then I succumbed and was so reduced by it that I became a whole catarrh myself, drawn to the ultimate thinness.[15] Often I had the impulse to end my life, but the old age of my devoted father restrained me. You see, I thought not of how bravely I could die, but of how he wouldn't be able to bear the loss bravely. So I commanded myself to live. Sometimes, after all, even to live is to do something brave.

I will tell you what I found comforting at that time, if I may say this first: the things thanks to which I calmed down had the power of medicine. Honourable comforts became a remedy, and whatever controlled the mind was as much of a benefit to the body. Our studies were salutary to me: I consider that it is because of philosophy that I rallied, that I recovered: I owe nothing less than my life to it. My friends did much to bring me to a good recovery – I was assuaged by their encouragements, their vigils and their conversation. Lucilius, best of men – nothing relieves and supports an invalid like the affection of friends, and nothing does more to tear away the anticipation and fear of death: it makes me think that when I leave my friends behind, I haven't died. I would add that I didn't think I would live with them, but *through* them. I didn't seem to be pouring my spirit out, but rather handing it on. This gave me the will to help myself and to endure every torment; and in any case, it is most wretched not to have the spirit for staying alive when you've got rid of the spirit for dying.[16]

The letter is not only about the possibility that the right sort of thinking can help to overcome disease, but also how it can make physical pain more bearable. Seneca is frank about what pain might await, but his remarks make clearer what he means when he says that we should neither be defeated by the pain, nor live solely for the purpose of enduring it. He is specific about what the worst sorts of pain are – he holds them to be in the leanest parts of the body, such as the nerves, the joints and other narrow passages – and optimistic about the prospect that the pain can be so bad that it can turn into numbness:

So this is the upside of great pain – that you inevitably stop feeling it if you feel it too much. But that is a problem for those who have no experience of physical discomfort: they are not used to being content in the soul – so much of their business is with the body. That's why great and sensible people treat their soul as separate from the body, and are much focused on the better, divine part, but only as much as necessary on the querulous, fragile part.[17]

Seneca is realistic about old age. He is an engaging writer on the subject because he knows himself, and his catarrhs and his fevers, and he knows the writings of others who have been there before. Like Cicero, he interacts with them: when he contemplates illness and the possibility of recovering from it, he quotes an often-repeated line of Virgil – 'one day, perhaps, the memory of even this will be a joy' – and we become aware of a spirit like that of Beethoven, who called a movement of his Op. 132 Quartet in A Minor 'an offering of thanks to the Godhead on recovery from sickness'. Seneca takes joy in his own writing without being indulgent – his style is spare, his letters seldom too long – and he somehow manages to demonstrate how to be old. A letter in which he realises, as if suddenly, that he is reaching old age, leads him to extol its own pleasures.[18] Here he follows Cicero, but adds some of the wine imagery that recurs with happy frequency throughout his corpus. Best of all, the letter shows how to crown a life:

Wherever I look, I see proofs of my old age. I had come to my suburban villa, and was complaining about the considerable disrepair of the building. The manager said that the problem wasn't because of his negligence, and that he had done all his tasks, but the house was old. This house grew in my care: what is to become of me, if the stones of my old age are as rotten?

In my anger I seized upon the next opportunity to vent my spleen at him. I said, 'These plane trees seem neglected; they don't have any leaves. The branches are so gnarled and parched, the trunks are so sad and rough. This wouldn't have happened if someone had dug around them and irrigated them.' He swore by Juno that he'd done everything, that his attention hadn't missed any detail; but they were old.

Entre nous, it was I who had planted them – I who had seen their first leaves. Turning to the door, I said, 'Who is that decrepit old man, understandably heading for his own exit? He's on the way out.[19] Where did you find him? What satisfaction is there for you in burying someone else's dead man?'

'Don't you recognise me?' he said. 'I'm Felicio – you used to bring me clay figurines. I'm the son of the old manager, Philositus, who was your dear friend.'

'Clearly the man's raving,' I said. 'My dear servant has become like a schoolboy again.[20] It could have happened – his teeth are falling out.'

I am indebted to my villa for making my old old age obvious wherever I turned. We should embrace it and love it. It is full of pleasure, if you know how to take it. Apples are most welcome when they are nearly over. Childhood is at its most becoming as it passes; the last sip from the wine delights its devotees – the sip that sinks them, that seals their drunkenness. The loveliest thing all pleasure has lingers until the end. A stage of life that is declining is the loveliest, rather than a full-on one. And I reckon that old age, reaching the last stage, has its own pleasures; or else, this one thing follows in place of pleasures: to need nothing. How pleasant it is to have exhausted desires, and to have left them . . .

. . . Heraclitus, whom an obscure style gave his nick-name,[21] said, 'One day is equal to all days.' Different people have taken this in different ways. Some say each day is equal in hours, and they're not wrong, because if a day is a period of 24 hours, then necessarily all days are the same as each other, because night takes what the day loses. But others say that one day has a similarity to all days, because the longest period of time has nothing in it that you wouldn't find in a single day, and in the changes of the world there are more things, but not different ones, just because one is longer and one is shorter. Therefore every day should be ordered as if it were the last in line – as if it consummated and fulfilled our life.

The governor Pacuvius, who made Syria his own by his exploitation of it, used to conduct the death-day celebrations with wine and appropriate funereal banquets,[22] being toted from dinner on a couch, while to applause the chant of eunuchs went up in harmony, 'Life's been lived! Life's been lived!' He bore himself off every day. What he was doing in bad conscience, we should do with a good one, and we should go to our sleep happy and cheery, saying, 'I lived – I ran the course that fortune gave.' If God were to give us a tomorrow, we should accept it happily. The most blessed and most secure people are the self-possessed ones who wait for tomorrow without anxiety. Whoever has said, 'I lived,' rises to a reward every day[23].

But now I must end my letter. You say, 'Does it come like this, with no little something for me?' Do not be afraid.[24] It brings something with it. Why did I say, 'Something'? It's a big thing. What is more distinguished than this pronouncement, which I hand on to you as something worth seeing through? 'It is bad to live in necessity; but it's not necessary to live in necessity.'[25] Why should it be necessary? Everywhere there are many quick, easy ways to freedom. Let us thank God that no one can be detained in a life – we are allowed to reject those very necessities.

'Epicurus said that!' you say. 'What are you doing with someone else's material?' If it's true, it's mine. I will keep

Epicurus working on you, so that those people who swear by speakers rather than valuing what they say might know that the best things are shared. Goodbye.

Seneca does argue, along with Cicero, that one pleasure of old age is not to need pleasure, and it's a mark of his rational approach that he can explain the joys to be had late in life so logically. He goes as far as to embrace that sense of finality and completion that old age can bring – the sense of the life reviewed – as its own pleasure.

Can we take anything from this?

This has not been an attempt to de-Christianise the debate about euthanasia, and in any case, just as a former archbishop can speak in favour of assisted dying, so distinguished clinicians can speak against it. Nor has it been an attempt to re-Christianise our thoughts on the afterlife. Seneca's views on suicide are not Christian, but his and Cicero's thoughts on the afterlife draw on the same Platonic ideas that inspired the early Christian thinkers.

Still, contemporary discussions of the end of life, and of how to end it, are moving away from Christianity. At least, if states are now able to debate laws such as the recent Assisted Dying Bill, which would allow mentally competent adults to request life-ending medication from a doctor if they have six months or less to live, then Christian ethics and the law are not the same. For an ancient, who doesn't have Christian ethics to consider, there is the question of demonstrating bravery, and of making a good end. Is it braver to continue a painful life, or to face the pain of a death you would inflict upon yourself? If the former is braver, what attitudes can sustain you towards the end? We often hear from the ancients that modesty of desire, of pleasure or expectation are helpful; mental activity can stave off decline of the memory and of thought; a life well lived is its own consolation. Seneca has even handed down his own way of feeling less pain.

And if the latter – suicide – is braver, then many ancients support it. The discovery of anaesthetics makes a big difference to our own discussion of suicide, but not in predictable ways. On the one hand, the ability to relieve pain is taken by some to make illness less distressing; but if we are missing that crucial sphere of mental activity, so prized by Seneca for its own sake, then the preservation of life can be a bitterness for those around us, with no end in sight. What answers we take from the ancients can depend on what answers we want, and knowing what we want has always been hard.

Conclusions

Throughout this discussion of ancient attitudes towards the elderly old age has been a bogeyman. The ancients personified old age – the Greeks made him a god, Geras, the son of night. He is depicted as a shrivelled old man, and in one red-figure *pelike* (a two-handled jar), Heracles is beating his naked frame with a club.

This is the kind of thing we do with illnesses: we make them seem like something else, something alien to us. We now know that some ancients, such as Aristotle and Seneca, really did see old age as an illness, but making Geras a figure of mockery didn't make him any less frightening. Horace called old age hateful – *invida* – just before writing the best-known two-word phrase in Latin.[1] He was picking up on couplings of words that seemed as natural to the Greeks, starting with Homer, who calls old age wretched in the *Odyssey* and hateful in the *Iliad*.[2] But every time the ancient Greeks heard that word, it echoed another word, *geras* with a shorter *e* sound; and that word meant honour. It's a link that Plutarch makes when he's arguing that the elderly should run the country.

So, if we had to caricature Geras the god based on what we have read about old age, what would he be like? He creeps up on us slowly but insistently. He approaches us at different times in our lives. He makes our speech softer and our brains wiser – as long as those brains can respond to what's going on and retain it. He changes our faces so that we may want to conceal his incursions or we may want to flaunt them. He may bring us ridicule, or he may bring us respect. He may free us from the pangs of desire; if he doesn't, he may still take away from the performance. He demands that we look after our parents. He makes us suspicious that our children will wrangle over our wills or, worse, that sharks beyond our families will seek our legacies.

So far, he's the baddy – a shrunken, dog-in-the-mangerish character who appears to resent anything we have and will snatch it away for no return. But what about the role of Geras in our careers, or in our mental activity, or in our deaths? Well, Plutarch says we should keep up with public life; Pliny the Younger says we should relax in old age; Cicero speaks of the old men who have served the state, and Seneca says we invite ridicule if we continue to work. As for our minds, Aristotle thinks that delirium can attack the elderly, while Cicero proposes ways to keep our thinking strong; Galen describes the symptoms of dementia, and a tale about Sophocles shows a man demonstrating his sanity to a packed court by declaiming his latest chorus. And when we approach our deaths, we can either confront Geras and bear his company, or else leave him and life itself.

On those occasions when we can demonise him, we end up looking like his victims: old age really does become an illness. But elsewhere the ancients present old age as an agency we can do something about. They tell us we can keep mentally and physically fit for as long as possible; that we can savour what pleasures are left to us; that we can look back on the past with as little shame as possible.

Cicero tries to exonerate Geras of his crimes. He blames the victims, and argues that if we find old age difficult, it's because of us and not because of old age. As we've remarked, this sounds bleak if we really are prey to a chronic condition or have been unable to rescue ourselves from bad decisions or difficult circumstances. But it's less depressing than something Franz Kafka said (as most things are): 'In the struggle between you and the world, back the world.' If old age is some kind of enemy, then Cicero is telling us not to be like Kafka, who assumes we're going to lose. We still have a chance of facing it with strength. And better still, there may be elements of it we can enjoy – the calmer pace, the less ravenous appetites, the opportunities to reflect, the enhanced kudos. These are the attributes of old age that allow us to think of *geras* with the short *e* – honour. Ultimately, old age is what we make of it, by which I don't just mean how we endure it, but also how we approach it and how we think of the elderly. If the world with which an old person struggles is really our perception of old age, then it's a world we can improve.

ON OLD AGE

Cicero on old age: a brief introduction

Moses Finley thought it incredible that Cicero's essay on old age has had such a hold on generations of readers. It's true that a new look at the work requires a little justification to today's audience, especially when our concerns about old age are often to do with the practical business of managing the money and the time needed for the care of an ageing population. The dialogue only briefly mentions resources, and this is to say that it's just as possible for the right sort of poor person to have a good old age as it is for somebody rich to be unhappy towards the end of life. We find a similar breezy logic in the assertions that if people are unhappy in old age, it's not old age's fault, but theirs: 'When Statius calls old men "stupid comic actors", he means the credulous, the forgetful, the careless – these are not the faults of old age, but of an inactive, lazy, drowsy old age.' This is not the voice of the more sympathetic Galen, who thinks of old age as something that attacks our natural constitution; nor of Seneca, who considers old age a disease in itself.

But those attitudes are just as depressing, with their sense that little can be done in the face of senescence, and Cicero is determined to take a more positive approach to ageing. His thinking becomes all the more positive when we consider the context in which he wrote it – the conditions of his own life and the intellectual and cultural environment in which he worked. And these factors may help to explain the fine and finished form in which the essay reaches us.

Cicero wrote this work in the weeks following the assassination of Julius Caesar. That happened on the ides of March, 44 BC; there is good reason to say that the book on old age was finished by May. Some think that the guarded words at the start, about the 'things that trouble you' and 'that trouble me more gravely still', reflect Cicero's fear of Mark Antony, who was already hounding those who sympathised with the assassins. Certainly Cicero had reasons to think that his own life could be coming to a quicker end, particularly since the feelings that Mark Antony was rousing against the senate and for the late dictator were aggressively against Cicero, who had done all he could to maintain Rome's republican constitution.

This was Cicero's last flurry of public engagement. Before then he had been an eye-catching, even reckless, lawyer, cajoling his audiences with invective, innuendo and lurid gossip while also climbing the ladder of public offices known as the *cursus honorum* – the track of honours provided by Rome's constitution – which led him to the crisis of his career: his election as consul in 63 BC. There were two consuls working together each year, and the role of the office was to lead the executive business of the state. When Cicero's turn came, there was a conspiracy to expose and a subsequent uprising to quell, both of which were down to the scheming of Catiline, a man whom Cicero was able to portray to the senate and to the people as a rich degenerate driven by his own ambitions. Cicero always thought of this moment as his triumph: the senate allowed him extraordinary powers to deal with the situation. But if we call it a career crisis, it's because he overplayed his hand. He firmly believed that the conspirators should be executed rather than exiled from Rome or placed under house arrest. His view prevailed in spite of more moderate voices in the senate, including Julius Caesar's, and the conspirators were strangled in prison. Four years after these events his opponents argued that he had abused his powers, and he went into exile.

Cicero's enforced withdrawal from public life led him to write philosophy, and, like Seneca and many others since, he found this a source of consolation and a kind of legacy he could leave once his political career had been curtailed. It's hard to resist the feeling that Cicero, who had occupied the offices of state almost as soon as the constitution allowed, had now become old before his time. His role model for the grandness of a grand old age, as we shall see, was Cato the Elder, who was still speaking in the senate and advising new generations of statesmen when in his eighties. Cicero, who peaked in his early forties and who, on his return, failed to dominate the senate as he had once done, was now reduced to writing letters and treatises in early retirement.

If 'reduced' sounds unfair, it's because his writing really did prove to be his legacy. In the run-up to the Renaissance it was the reading of Cicero that gave scholars their quickest route to Greek philosophy. In the dialogue on old age we constantly encounter his deep reading of Plato, to whom the book owes much of its content and form. And it was a genuine consolation. However much we may look at *On Old Age* as an empathetic glimpse of how the life review works and find glimpses of Cicero's own pride in having reached a pinnacle of public life, there is something more private going on, and perhaps more important. The year before composing the book Cicero lost his beloved daughter Tullia. In one of the crowning passages of *On Old Age* Cato anticipates that he will rejoin his own son. Such moments make the book's central ideas all the more intimate: why fear death more as an old person than you would as a young one, when it can come at any time? If you're worried about old age, live a youth of which you can be proud; and if you're worried about death, faith in the immortality of the soul will assuage your fear.

To understand Cicero's readiness to adopt the persona of Cato the Elder, we need to know more about Cato himself. One clue is in the name – the Elder. In Latin the book is called *Cato Maior de Senectute*, and the elision between 'elder' and 'greater' is instinctive in Latin. Like Cicero, he had occupied positions on the *cursus honorum*, including consul. The one for which Cato was best remembered was the last he held – the role of censor, in which he established himself as a guardian of public morals and championed Roman values above Greek ones. The lengths he went to in order to do this could be surprising: for example, as consul he wanted to retain a law that prevented women from wearing excessive jewellery or too-fancy clothes. (The Oppian law had come into force during the wars against Carthage, the idea being that domestic austerity would support the cost of campaigning abroad.) The idea of Bacchic cults, so much a feature of Athens's golden age, gave him conniptions. Cato came from Sabine origins – from a people proverbially known for their rustic, hardy, no-frills attitudes – and Cicero has to work hard to persuade his readers that Cato could have engaged as willingly with Greek culture as he does in the pages of *On Old Age*. Still, Cicero's Cato stands for Ciceronian things: moderation, tradition, the constitution, simplicity and farming.

So is Cato here really Cicero? I'm not always sure. As Mary Beard has recently pointed out in her work on Roman humour, Cicero was often regarded as a funny man, however surprising that may be to those who have had to translate him unseen in exams. There are passages of *On Old Age* that are entertaining, and the humour is quite likely to be knowing. What, for example, are we to make of a man who refers to his own book on agriculture with 'What should I say about the effectiveness of manuring?' This is during a digression about agriculture that goes on long enough for Cato as if accidentally to return to the original subject of old age, only to tick himself off for straying from the subject of farming.

It's possible that moments such as having Cato say, 'But back to me. I'm 84 years old,' may not be a caricature of an elderly person who constantly reminds us of his or her age; and Cato saying a second time, 'But why am I talking about other people? Let me go back to talking about myself,' may not be a sop to Aristotle's view that the elderly are self-obsessed people who talk incessantly about the past. But Cicero does make Cato aware of the tendency. In the middle of his ramble through the world of farming he gently mocks his whole treatise by saying, 'Old age is naturally loquacious (I shouldn't look like I'm exonerating it totally).' Towards the end of *On Old Age*, Cato remarks, 'If I might boast about myself a little in the manner of the elderly, do you think I would have undertaken such great tasks, either at home or on the battlefield, if the endpoint of my life would also be the limit of my fame?'

In fact, the whole design and execution of the book makes points about the elderly. Yes, Cato the Elder is constantly name-dropping and flexing his intellectual muscles with the kind of gymnastics with which the ancients still impress us: the ability to remember who did what when whoever it was was consul, or to work out how likely it was that some table talk from Plato could have been accurately related by generations of anecdotalists between the time of Plato's birth and Cato's childhood. Cicero makes his speaker a character from a hundred years before, and that character in turn takes a scholarly view of the hundreds of years before him, and Cato himself is allowed to take his wisdom from the other elderly people he has known. When reading this, let alone when translating it, it's tempting to skip over these parts as being too full of number crunching and mulling over the deeds and reputations of bit players who would be lucky to have a stub on Wikipedia, but this would be to miss the point. Cato's onstage audience must sit patiently through this business, and will do so in an awareness that it's only thanks to dignified and learned old souls to come that they will ever be remembered in their turn.

Seen this way, even the structure of *On Old Age* is part of a tradition. It is constructed as a dialogue of the sort Plato wrote, with one source of wisdom – in this case Cato the Elder – and two characters who have much to learn but at least have the intelligence to realise that if they want to learn it, they have come to the right place. And what these speakers say is also a straight lift from Plato: they as good as repeat the opening of the *Republic*, while the passages about the immortality of the soul draw heavily on the *Phaedo*, in which Socrates faces his execution and comforts his followers by sharing his excitement about the life to come. What's more, within the Greek structure of the dialectic dialogue Cicero lets Cato construct his arguments in the order that a forensic orator would prescribe: introduce the territory of your debate; list some erroneous assumptions about your case; refute them one by one by using a wealth of evidence alongside your own personal experience; conclude with an appeal to the audience. So Cato lists four common canards about old age, each of which he demolishes, before hoping that the two young men who have heard it can use this wisdom when their own turn comes to grow old.

It's the elegance of this structure that makes it so distinctly a work of Cicero's, and it's tempting to see Cicero signing off on his literary career by doing what he does best – flattening his opponents with scholarship and rhetoric. The appeal to the past may seem nostalgic, reactionary or even simply desperate, but we need constantly to bear in mind what Cicero was facing: bereavement, the prospect of his life's work coming to nothing, the possibility of a violent vindictive death, and then old age itself – an old age in antiquity. Cicero turned to those who were ancient to him when seeking a guide on how to grow old, and if his method of assuaging his own fears makes us in turn look at our own ancients, then, for better or for worse, it's what he would have wanted.

A brief note on the translation

To students of the language Cicero has always been the model of how to write Latin prose, and the effect of reading it has rubbed off on English writers too – speech makers may still be called Ciceronian, and in the law courts, where Cicero made his name as a speaker, we can still hear his impact in a dramatic summing-up or a colourful character assassination. As a result, it's hard not to make him sound formal, and there's a risk that a translation can tip him over into stuffiness. This would be unfortunate, not so much because it's always worth considering the possibility that he may have something to say to new readers, but because it's not all that often how Cicero sounds. As a legal orator, however interested he is in the law, he's just as taken up with gossip, with mockery and even with sarcasm, and as a philosopher he regularly uses the form of the dialogue, which on the one hand pays homage to his Greek model Plato, and on the other allows an atmosphere of intimacy and reflection.

This is especially true of *On Old Age*. For all that it is constructed as a legal argument, with claims and counterclaims, Cicero does allow Cato to do jokes, and these are of a congenial, self-deprecating kind. He even allows some gentle wordplay. In response to this, I have tried – not always successfully, maybe, but tried – to maintain a conversational air in this translation. This has sometimes meant re-punctuating, or splitting sentences into two, or bringing subjects closer to their objects, or repeating nouns so that the Latin pronouns have to work less hard or can govern shorter clauses.

It's worth remembering that Cicero's achievement as a philosopher was not so much in coming up with original ideas as in preserving the thought of the Greeks. His fellow Romans were already familiar with these ideas, so the real value of Cicero's work was to come when Europeans lost their Greek in the centuries before the Renaissance. To medieval scholars, Cicero was one of the most effective links to Platonic and Stoic ideas. If this in itself seems more like an accident of history than an achievement in its own right, we should bear in mind that Latin has nothing like the flexibility of the Greek language, nor its massive vocabulary. For this reason, it's not often desirable or even possible to find a word in English that is the equivalent of a Latin word each time it appears; and readers who are tempted to use this version as a crib should bear that in mind, along with other ticks or deficiencies.

Cato the Elder on Old Age

Cicero begins his treatise with a dedication to his friend Atticus; the opening lines of verse are by Ennius, said to be a friend of Cato's.

Titus, if I could help, and could relieve
the care that cooks you, turning in your chest,
what would be my reward?

1. You see, I have known the moderation and calm of your mind, and understand that it's not only your name that comes from Athens, but also your humanity and good sense. And yet I suspect that you are perturbed by the same things that trouble me more gravely still; their consolation is at once greater and should be put off for another time. But now it seems that I should write something for you about old age.

2. I want to free both you and myself from this burden, which we both share, of old age, whether it is pressing or inevitably approaching; even though I know for sure that you are bearing it, and will bear it, as you do everything, proportionately and wisely. Still, you strike me as worthy of this gift, which can be useful to the pair of us alike. In fact, putting this book together was

114

such a pleasing thing to do that it will not only have wiped away the troubles of old age, but even made old age gentle and pleasing. So philosophy can never be given enough of its due praise, since whoever is observant of it can live out any stage of his life untroubled.[1]

3. But I've said a lot about everything else, and will often say it: this book that I'm sending you is about old age. I've ascribed a whole speech not to Tithonus, as Aristo Cius does (because there would be too little authority in a myth),[2] but to the old man Marcus Cato, from whom the speech would have had greater authority; at his house I've made Laelius and Scipio marvel that he bears old age so easily, and I've made him reply to them. If he seems to argue with more erudition than he usually did in his books, then I attribute this to the Greek literature of which he was known to be a devoted student in his old age. But who needs more explanation? Now, Cato's own speech will explain all my thinking about old age.

4. *Scipio*: Like Gaius Laelius here, I am often in the habit of admiring your excellent and thorough wisdom in other things, and particularly that I never feel that old age, which is so odious to most old men that they say they are holding up a burden heavier than Mount Etna, is hard for you.[3]

Cato: Scipio, Laelius, you seem to admire something that is hardly difficult. To those who don't have the means of living well and happily, every age is hard; but to those who look within themselves for all good things, nothing that the necessity of nature brings can seem bad. A prime example of this sort of thing is old age, which everyone wants to achieve, and which, once it's achieved, they rebuke; that's how inconsistent and perverse their stupidity is. They say it crept up more quickly than they would have thought. First, who made them believe this falsehood? In what way does old age creep up on youth more quietly then? And then, would old age be any less hard if these people lived to be 800 rather than 80? Once it's gone, no age range, however long, can soothe foolish old age with any consolation.

5. So, if you are in the habit of admiring my wisdom – and if only it were worthy of your estimation and my family name – I am wise in this: that I follow nature as a leader and obey it as if it were a god; and since the scenes of the rest of life are so well scripted, it seems unlikely that nature would neglect the last act as though she were a lazy author. Still, there needs to be something at the very end, and, withered and about to fall as it is, like the berries of the trees or the fruits of the earth it should be borne calmly by the wise. After all, what is fighting with gods, in the manner of giants, if not rebuffing nature?

6. *Laelius*: Yes, Cato, but since we hope (and really want) to become old men, you would do us a great favour (I'm sure I speak for Scipio too) if we could learn from you long in advance the thinking by which we can bear the growing weight of old age more easily.

Cato: I'll certainly do that, Laelius, especially if it is going to be welcome to both of you, as you say.

Laelius: If it isn't a bother, Cato, we really would like to see what kind of place you have reached, because you have gone a long way down the road that we too must take.

7. *Cato*: I'll do what I can, Laelius. The thing is, I often heard the complaints that my peers used to make (like gathers with like, as the old saying goes) – ex-consuls and men nearly my age such as Gaius Salinator and Spurius Albinus – that they lacked pleasures, and without these they didn't think life was anything,[4] and then that they were spurned by the people who used to seek their company; and these men seemed to blame what they shouldn't have blamed. You see, if that were old age's fault, then in fact the same things would come to me and all other older people, many of whom I have seen bear old age without complaint – who, without fuss, felt freed from the chains of their desires and were not shunned by those around them. But the blame for all complaints of this kind lies in character and not in age. So moderate people, and the elderly who aren't stubborn or indecent, lead a tolerable old age, whereas insolence and indecency are problems for every age group.

8. *Laelius*: What you say is true, Cato, although perhaps someone would say that your old age seems more bearable to you because of your wealth, resources and standing; but for many people that can't be the case.

Cato: There is something in that, Laelius, but by no means everything; as Themistocles is supposed to have retorted to some Seriphian during a row, when the Seriphian said that Themistocles' glamour came from his country's glory rather than his own: 'Listen, I'd never have been famous if I'd been from Seriphos, and you wouldn't have been if you'd come from Athens.'[5] You can talk about old age in the same way because it can't be easy even for somebody wise if they're in a state of utter destitution, and can be severe to fools even if they enjoy the height of affluence.

9.   All in all, the best weapons old age has are the skills and practice of virtue, and if they are cultivated at all ages, they can bear marvellous fruit if you live a long and full life, not only because they never leave you – not even at the very end of age, even though that is momentous – but also because the knowledge of a life well lived and of many deeds well done is a complete joy.

10.   When I was a young man, I revered the old man Quintus Maximus – who recaptured Tarentum – as if he were an equal.[6] He had a gravity tempered by companionship, and old age didn't change his character. Although I began to seek him out when he was not yet of great age, he was at any rate getting on. You see, it was in the year after I was born that he was consul for the first time; and during his fourth consulate, when I was a very young man[7] I set out with him as a soldier, to Capua, and five years later to Tarentum. In four years' time I was appointed quaestor, and I conducted my business as a magistrate when Tuditanus and Cethegus were consuls, and Quintus Maximus, although an old man, was an advocate of Cincia's law about gifts and payments.[8] This was a man who fought a war as if he were a youth when he was obviously aged, and with his patience he tamed a boyishly gloating Hannibal. My friend Ennius memorably writes about that:

> One man restored the state by his delay,
> not valuing vulgar gossip more than safety;
> so glory now distinguishes him more.

11. And really, he recaptured Tarentum with such patience and such planning! In my hearing, when the boasting Salinator, who had fled to the citadel from the lost town, said, 'Quintus Maximus, you have recaptured Tarentum thanks to my efforts,' he replied, laughing, 'Absolutely – if you hadn't lost it, I wouldn't have retaken it.'

And he was no less outstanding when wearing his armour than when wearing the toga: when he was again consul (and his fellow consul Spurius Carvilius was remaining neutral) he put up as much resistance as possible to the tribune of the people, Caius Flaminius, who was dividing up the Picene and Gallic lands among individual men against the will of the senate; and although he was an augur, he dared to say that things done for the safety of the state were done under the best auspices, and things done against the state were done against the auspices.[9] I saw many distinctions in that man, but nothing was more admirable than the way he bore the death of his son, a remarkable man and a consul.[10] We have access to the eulogy, and when we read it, is there any philosopher we wouldn't scorn? Really, he wasn't only great in plain sight and in the eyes of the people, but he was even more outstanding in his private and domestic life. What great conversation! What great advice! What a regard for the past, and what knowledge of augurial law! He was well read, for a Roman – he had by memory not only all the internal wars, but also the external ones. I eagerly relished his conversation, as if I were foreseeing what actually happened – that when he was dead, there would be no one from whom I could learn anything.

13. So why have I said so much about Maximus? Well, it's clearly outrageous to say that an old age like his was miserable. But not everyone can be a Scipio or a Maximus, able to remember the captures of cities, the battles on land and sea, the wars he's waged, the triumphs. Even so, there is still the calm, gentle old age of a life lived out quietly and purely – tastefully too – like Plato's, we understand, who died in his eighty-first year, still writing; like the old age of Isocrates, who said that he wrote the book called *Panathenaicus* in his ninety-fourth year, and who lived for five years after that.[11] And his teacher, Gorgias of Leontini, lived out 107 years without ceasing in his study or labour.[12] When someone asked him why he would want to stay alive so long, he said, 'I don't have anything for which I could blame old age.' A fine answer worthy of a learned man.

14. So fools attribute their own weaknesses, and their own sin, to old age, which is something Ennius didn't do (I mentioned him earlier):

Like a strong horse who'd reach the finish line
Olympic victor, tired by age, he rests.

He compares his old age to that of the victorious horse. You probably remember him because nineteen years after his death Titus Flaminius and Manius Cilius were made consuls,[13] and he died when Philip was again consul, with Caepio – when I, aged 65, spoke in favour of Volconius' law with a big voice and good lungs.[14] But at the age of 70 (which is how long Ennius lived) he bore the two burdens that are thought the biggest – poverty and old age – so that he almost seemed to delight in them.

15. So then when I list them in my mind, I find four reasons why old age might seem miserable:

> One, because it calls us away from things worth doing;
> Two, because it makes the body weaker;
> Three, because it deprives us of nearly all pleasures;
> Four, because it isn't far from death.

Let's look at these one by one to see how fair they are.

Old age pulls us away from things worth doing. From what? From things to do in robust youth? So is there nothing that old people, although physically infirm, can manage with their spirit and brain? Was Quintus Maximus doing nothing, or Lucius Paulus, your father and father-in-law of that great man, my son? When those other old men were defending the state with their advice and authority – the likes of Fabricius, Curius, Coruncanius – were they doing nothing?

16. Blindness befell the old age of Appius Claudius;[15] but when the mood of the senate was leaning towards peace, and making a treaty with Pyrrhus, he didn't hesitate to say what Ennius has explored in his verse:

> O you, whose minds had stood so firm before –
> Why are you mad enough to bend your course?

. . . and so on, severely – after all, you know the poem, and Appius' speech is available. And he said this seventeen years after his second consulship, when there had been ten years between the two terms of office, and he had been censor before he was consul, which is how we know he was rather mature at the time of the war with Pyrrhus – at least, that's what we understand from our fathers.

17. So it's pointless when people say that old age has nothing to contribute to the running of affairs; they are like those who say that a helmsman contributes nothing to sailing, quietly sitting in the stern and holding the tiller when others are climbing masts, running across decks or manning pumps. He doesn't do what young people do, but really he's doing things that are much bigger and better. Great things are done not by haste or bodily speed, but by counsel, authority, thought. It's not just that old age isn't deprived of these things; they actually increase.

18. That is, unless it seems to you that I have have stopped, since, having been a soldier, captain, ambassador and consul in a range of conflicts, I am no longer waging war. And yet, I guide the senate on what should be done, and how it should be done. Far in advance, I am declaring war on Carthage (which has been devising wicked plans for a while), and I fear I will not stop before I know that Carthage is razed to the ground. I pray that the gods can keep a crown for you, Scipio, so that you can complete your grandfather's legacy.[16] It has been thirty-three years since his death, but the passing years will welcome the memory of that hero.

He died in the year before I was censor, and nine years after I was consul – when I was consul, he was elected as consul again.

19. So if he had lived into his hundredth year, would he be complaining about his old age? Well, he wouldn't be practising his running or jumping or using his spears from a distance, or swords up close; but he would be exercising his counsel, his reason, his thought, which, if they weren't the attributes of our seniors, our fore-fathers wouldn't have called our highest governing body 'Senate'.[17]

20. Among the Spartans those who hold the most honour-able office are called 'elders', because they are.[18] If you want to read or hear about foreign affairs, you find that states are overthrown by the young, but sustained and restored by the old. 'I put it to you – how did you lose such a great state so quickly?' That's what they demand to know in the play *Ludius* by Naevius the poet. There are many answers, but principally this one: 'New orators stepped up – stupid young men.' Clearly, the feature of blooming youth is chutzpah; in old age it's prudence.

21. But then there's the fading memory. I believe there is, unless you exercise it or if you're slower by nature. Themistocles memorised the names of every citizen;[19] as he advanced in age, surely you don't imagine that he would address Aristides as Lysimachus? To be sure, I know not only those who are alive now, but also their fathers and even grandfathers – and I don't worry that I'll lose my memory while reading the inscriptions on their graves. By reading them I refresh my memory of the dead. And I never heard of an old man who'd

forgotten where he'd hidden his treasure. The elderly remember everything they care about: the dates of court hearings; to whom they owe money; who owes it to them.[20]

22. What about old men as lawyers, priests, soothsayers and philosophers? They remember so much! Old men keep their wits as long as their zeal and industry remains, which is true not only of the man with a life of distinction and public service but also with a private, withdrawn life. Sophocles wrote his tragedies at the peak of old age: when he seemed to be neglecting his family affairs because of his work, he was summoned to court by his sons so that the jury could bar him from family business as if he were of unsound mind (just as it's common for fathers to be banned from managing their affairs by our own law). We're told that then the old man recited his forthcoming play, which he was working on – *Oedipus at Colonus* – and asked how that poetry could be by someone of unsound mind; and after the recitation he was acquitted by the judgement of the jury.

23. Did old age force him to be silent from his work? Or Homer, Hesiod, Simonides, Stesichorus, or Isocrates (whom I mentioned) or those princes of philosophy Pythagoras, Democritus, Plato, Xenocrates or, later, Zeno, Cleanthes or Diogenes the Stoic whom you have seen in Rome? Or rather, did their action in these endeavours last as long as their lives?

24. Let's move on and skip those exalted labours: I can name rustic Romans in the Sabine fields – friends and neighbours of mine – who are almost never away from

farm work of any importance: not from sowing, not from harvesting, not from storing the crop. In some matters this isn't so surprising, since no one is so old that he doesn't think he can live another year; but the same people work on things which they know have absolutely nothing to do with them: 'he plants the trees to help another age', as our compatriot Statius says in his comedy *The Young Comrades*.

25. And if you ask a farmer, no matter how old he is, whom he's planting for, he won't hesitate to reply, 'For the immortal gods, who wanted me not only to accept these things from my ancestors, but also to extend them to posterity.'

Statius put it better then, on the subject of an old man anticipating another generation, than in the following:

Old age, by God – if you brought just one trouble
along with you, this one would be enough:
the long-lived see what they don't want to see.

And perhaps there's much they do like; for that matter, even adolescence can often run into things it doesn't want. Statius wrote this, even more feebly:

I reckon what is worst about old age is, thinking the next generation hates you.[21]

26. Rejoices in, rather than hates! After all, just as wise old people delight in young people who are gifted with innate goodness, and the old age of those who are cultivated and admired by the young is easier, so young

people cherish the advice of the old, which leads them to strivings for virtue;[22] and I don't believe that I'm less of a joy to you than you are to me. But you see not only that old age isn't languid and inactive, but also that it's always busy; it's always doing something, that is to say, coming up with the kind of thing for which it was striving in an earlier part of life.[23] And what about those who keep on adding things – as we see in the case of Solon, who exulted in his poetry and said that he became old learning something new every day? I've been doing this too: as an old man, I have been studying Greek literature, which I've snatched up as if longing to quench a lingering thirst, so that I can know the material that I'm now using for my examples.[24] Then when I heard that Socrates had done this with the lyre, I really wanted to do that, too, because the ancients used to learn the lyre; but I've certainly worked hard on literature.

27. **And I don't feel that I lack the strength of youth – because that was the second point about the deficiencies of old age** – any more than I used to long for the strength of a bull or an elephant when I was a young man. It is right that you should use what strength you have and do whatever your strength allows you to do. After all, what speech can be more contemptible than Milo of Crotona's? When he was already an old man, watching the athletes exercising on the track, he is supposed to have looked at his own muscles and said through his tears, 'And yet these ones are dead.' But they're nothing like as dead as you, you lightweight, because nothing celebrated ever came from you yourself, but from your lungs and your muscles. Sextus Aelius

was nothing like that, nor Titus Coruncanius from many years before that, nor, later, Publius Crassus: they used to pronounce on legal matters to the citizens; their prudence prevailed to their last breath.

28. I fear that the orator does languish in old age because his gift is not only his wit, but also his lungs and physical strength. No doubt what charm the voice has can gleam in old age (who knows how); for sure, I haven't lost it, and you know how old I am. But still, a soft, relaxed tone befits an old man, and often it's that considered, gentle speech that makes people listen;[25] and even if you cannot be a speaker, you can still give advice to a Scipio or a Laelius.

29. Because what is more pleasant than old age surrounded by the zeal of youth? Or do we not grant to old age even the strength needed to teach and train the young, and prepare them for every public duty? What could be more distinguished than this task? For me, Gnaeus Scipio, Publius Scipio, and your two grandfathers, Lucius Aemilius and Publius Africanus, seemed lucky to have the companionship of noble young men; and no teachers of the liberal arts should be considered anything but blessed, even if their physical powers may be ageing and failing.

And yet it's precisely this failure of strength that is brought on by the weaknesses of youth, because lustful, immoderate youth hands on a worn-out body to old age.

30. For example, according to Xenophon, when Cyrus was a really old man, he said in a conversation he was holding as he died that he never felt any feebler in his

old age than he had felt in his youth. As a boy I remember Lucius Metellus, who was appointed High Priest four years after his second consulship, and held that priesthood for twenty-two years: he had such great strength in the last phase of his life that he didn't miss his youth. There is no need for me to talk about myself, although that is a right for the elderly, and is given to people of my age.

31. You know how frequently Homer has Nestor hold forth about his own strengths? Well, he was witnessing a third generation of men, and wasn't worried that he would seem too rude or verbose by telling the truth about himself. As Homer says, 'Sweeter than honey flowed speech from his tongue'; and that smoothness needed no physical strength. In any case, the Greek leader never wishes he had ten men like Ajax, but like Nestor instead, and he had no doubt that if that had been his lot then Troy would have collapsed rapidly.

32. But back to me. I'm 84 years old. I'd like to be able to boast as Cyrus did, but I can at least say this: that while I don't have the strength I had as a soldier in the war against Carthage, or as a quaestor[26] in the same war, or when I was a consul in Spain or when I saw the campaign through as military tribune at Thermopylae four years after that (when Manius Glabrio was consul), nevertheless, old age hasn't shaken my nerve or laid me low, as you can plainly see. The senate doesn't go without me, nor the speaker's platform, nor my friends, nor followers, nor guests. And I've never agreed with the much-praised quotation of the old man who advised that you should become old early if you want to be old for a long

time.[27] Me, I'd rather have a shorter old age than to be old before my time. So I've never turned away anyone who wanted to consult me because I was busy.

33. Still, I have less strength than either of you. But you don't have the strength of Centurion Titus Pontius. Does that make him any better than you? Let there be moderation in the use of strength, and let each man strive as much as he can – that way, he won't be afflicted by severe loss of it. We're told that Milo of Crotona marched along the Olympic track carrying an ox on his shoulders. Which of these would you rather have – that physical strength, or the intellect of Pythagoras? Ultimately, you should use the advantage when you have it and not miss it when you don't, unless young people somehow ought to miss their childhood, or miss their youth when they advance in age. The track of life is fixed; nature has one road, and it's direct. Each stage of life has its own season, so that childhood naturally has its dependency, youth its ardour, middle age its seriousness, and old age its maturity. You should welcome each in its time.

34. Scipio, I think you hear about the daily activities of your grandfather's host, the 90-year-old Masinissa: that when he makes a journey on foot, he absolutely doesn't mount a horse, but if he goes by horse, he doesn't get off it; that there's no shower or cold that can make him go with his head covered; that there is peak dryness[28] in his body so he can carry the duties of his kingly office. So exercise and restraint can preserve for the elderly something of their former strength.

If we assume that there is no strength in old age, then no strength is demanded of it. So, by law and custom, our old age vacates those offices which we can't conduct without strength.[29] As a result, we're not driven to do what we can't do, nor even what we can't do as fully as we can.

35. And yet there are many old people who are so feeble that they can carry out no official function and none of life's duties either. Still, even that is not a property of old age, but of poor health in general. Scipio – the man who adopted you, Publius Africanus – was feeble, with such tenuous health, or rather no health. If he hadn't been that way, he might have stood out as a second beacon of the state – to his father's breadth of intellect he would have added still more fruitful learning. So is it any wonder that there should be some ailments in the elderly when not even young people are able to escape them?

Laelius, Scipio – we need to fight back against old age. Its weaknesses need counterbalancing with diligence. We should combat sickness and old age in the same way.

36. We should have a fitness regime; we should undertake moderate exercise; we should take in just so much food and drink as will refresh our strength rather than oppress it.[30] And really it's not just the body that needs support – the mind and the spirit require even more; because old age extinguishes these too, if you don't add oil to the lamp. And while bodies slump with the fatigue of exercise, exercise lifts the spirits. When Statius calls old men 'stupid comic actors', he means the credulous, the forgetful, the careless – these are not the faults of old age, but of an inactive, lazy, drowsy old age.[31] Just as petulance and lust are greater among the young than

the old, but not characteristic of all young people, but just the bad ones, so the stupidity of the old, which is often called delirium, is characteristic not of all old people, but just the silly ones.

37. Even when he was old and blind, Appius managed four strapping sons, five daughters, a fine household and a large retinue, because his mind was taut as a bow, and he didn't give in to old age as a dotard. He retained not only his authority but also his command over his circle: his slaves feared him; his children respected him; everyone held him dear. Tradition and discipline flourished in his house.

38. So old age is honourable if it takes care of itself, if it keeps its own law, is beholden to no one, and is in control of its own affairs right up to the last breath.[32] That's why I approve of the young person who has something of the elderly about him, and the old person in whom there's a bit of youth − because someone observing this may be old in body but never in mind.

I am now working on my seventh volume of histories [*Origines*];[33] I am collecting all the records of the past; I am thoroughly polishing the speeches I made in famous court cases; I am studying civil and religious law, and the laws of augury; I'm greatly engaged with Greek literature; and to keep my memory exercised every evening I recall whatever I've said, heard and done that day, as was the habit of Pythagoras. These are the exercises of the intellect and the racetracks of the mind. By sweating through these workouts, I don't much miss my physical strength. I am there for my friends; I go cramming into the senate, where I propose my own long-considered motions, using the strength of my mind rather than my body. Even if I couldn't do these things, I would have the joy my couch gives me,[34] of thinking about the things I can no longer do; and it's because of the life I've lived that I can do that. You see, to someone who lives in these pursuits and labours, it's never clear when old age creeps up on them; this way, life ages softly, imperceptibly – not suddenly snapped, but eventually snuffed out.

39. **Next, the third insult to old age – that it lacks pleasures.** Oh, what an amazing gift of old age, if it takes from us what is most deplorable about youth! You distinguished young men should really take in that old speech by that especially great, wonderful man, Archytas of Tarentum. I heard about it when I was a young man serving at Tarentum with Quintus Maximus. Archytas said that nature has afflicted human bodies with no plague greater than pleasure, because pleasure urges desires rashly and uncontrollably towards their slaking.[35]

40. This is where treason and revolution are born, and conspiracy with the enemy; ultimately, there is no crime, no evil deed that the lust for pleasure hasn't provoked. That's right: rape, adultery and every offence of that type are incited by nothing but the temptation of pleasure, and since nature, or some god, has given men nothing more outstanding than the mind, there is nothing more hostile to this divine gift and responsibility than pleasure.

41. There is no room for temperance when lust is oppressive, and virtue can't exist in the kingdom[36] of pleasure.

To make himself better understood, Archytas told us to imagine someone aroused by as much pleasure as he could take, and he argued that it would be indisputable that while that person was in those throes, he wouldn't be able to operate mentally[37] or be capable of reason and imagination. It follows that there is nothing so loathsome and infectious as pleasure, especially if it is intense and enduring enough to put out all your mental lights. Nearchus, my host in Tarentum, who maintained his friendship with the Roman people, said that he learned this as a child from his elders, and that Archytas had spoken it in conversation with Pontius of Samnium (father of the man who defeated Spurius Postumius and Titus Veturius at the Battle of the Caudine Forks), and that Plato was involved in the exchange, and I've established that Plato went to Tarentum when Lucius Camillus and Appius Claudius were consuls.[38]

42. So what's this for? To make you understand that if we can't rebuff pleasure with reason and wisdom, then we should be grateful to old age, which makes sure that we are not free to do what we shouldn't do. The fact is that pleasure inhibits forethought, opposes reason and, in a manner of speaking, covers up the mind's eyes; it has no interaction with virtue.[39]

I was reluctant when I expelled Lucius Flaminius from the senate (his brother was Titus, that bravest of men, and Lucius had been consul seven years before), but his lust was damnable. You see, when he was consul and in Gaul, a whore encouraged him to take an axe to one of the prisoners on death row. With his brother Titus as censor (just before I was), Lucius escaped judgement, but to me and Flaccus such outrageous and abandoned desire was impossible to condone when it combined a crime against an individual with the disrepute of the state.

43. I've often heard from our elders (who in turn said that they were boys when they heard it from the old) that Caius Fabricius used to marvel at what he heard, while serving as ambassador to King Pyrrhus, from Cineas of Thessaly: that there was a man from Athens who professed that he was wise, and who said that everything we do should be gauged according to pleasure. And when Marcus Curius and Tiberius Coruncanius heard this, they would often wish that they could recommend it to the Samnites and to Pyrrhus himself, who would be more beatable once they'd given themselves to pleasure. During his fourth consulship (and five years before his companion Manius Curius was consul) Publius Decius gave himself as a sacrifice on behalf of the state.[40] Fabricius knew him, as did Coruncanius, and because of their own lives and the action of Decius that I've mentioned, they concluded that some things can be so fine and wonderful in their nature that they are worth seeking for their own sake, and which the best of men will pursue with a scornful dismissal of pleasure.

44. So why have I said so much about pleasure? It's because saying that old age doesn't greatly miss any pleasures is not an insult to it, but the highest praise. Old age goes without the banquet, the heaped-up table, the never-empty cup, and so it goes without drunkenness, indigestion and insomnia. But if we can concede anything to pleasure – since its blandishments aren't easy to resist

(which is why Plato was inspired when he called pleasure 'the bait of evil', clearly because it catches men as if they were fish) – it's this: although old age goes without immoderate feasts, it can still enjoy modest dinner parties. As a boy I would often see the old man Caius Duellius returning from supper (he was the son of Marcus and the first Roman to beat the Carthaginians at sea). On his way he was delighted by the torchlight and flute player: he assumed the right to these things although there was no precedent; his fame allowed him that much indulgence.

45. But why am I talking about other people? Let me go back to talking about myself. For a start, I have always had friends in societies[41] – in fact the societies honouring Cybele were set up when I was quaestor – so I would feast with these friends, with great moderation, but there was still that fervour which belongs to my age – as that age advances, so everything becomes more gentle by the day. And I didn't count the joy of those banquets' physical pleasures more highly than the joy of friends meeting up and talking. Our ancestors wisely called a feast on couches among friends a 'convivium', because it entails a sharing of life, which is better than the Greeks, who called the same thing a 'symposium' (drinking together) and also a 'syndeipnum' (dining together), so that they seem to applaud most highly the thing that is least important in that kind of gathering.

46. In fact, I used to enjoy the delights of those dinners that started early,[42] not only with my peers, few of whom are alive now, but also with you and with people of your age, and I am most grateful to old age that it

has increased my hunger for conversation and taken away the appetite for food and drink. But if anyone does enjoy those things (and I don't want to look as though I have declared war on pleasure completely, because perhaps a natural amount of it is allowed), then I don't see that old age really is so totally numb to those particular pleasures. In fact, I delight in those dinners our ancestors founded, with toastmasters; and in the conversation which, according to tradition, starts when the drinking starts at the top of the table; and in the small, sprinkled cups like the ones in Xenophon's *Symposium*, which are a refreshment in summer and like the sun and a fire in winter. Even when I'm with the Sabines it's my habit to follow this way of life, and every day I make up a party with my neighbours, which we stretch out with a range of conversation as deep into the night as we can.

47. But there is not so much of pleasure's titillation for old men. I do believe that, but there's not so much longing either: what you don't miss can't bother you. When he was an old man, Sophocles put it well when someone asked him if he still enjoyed sex. 'Good heavens! I've run away from that, as if from a crude and raging master.' The lack of such things is perhaps unpleasant and annoying to someone who wants them, but to someone who's sated and glutted with them, it's better to lack them than to enjoy them.[43] If you don't miss something, you're not going without it – which is why I say that you are happier if you're not missing it.

48. But what if someone in the bloom of youth[44] enjoys those same pleasures more indulgently? Well, first, he's

enjoying trivial things; and then, although old age doesn't have such a range of pleasures available to it, it doesn't altogether lack them. Just as the spectator in the front row of the theatre enjoys a performance of Ambivius Turpio more but the spectator at the back enjoys it too, in the same way, youth is perhaps happier looking at pleasures at closer quarters, but looking at them from further away is cheering enough.

49. But how valuable is the soul that's demobbed from the battle of lust and ambition, of rivalry and hostility, to uncouple itself (as people say) from all desire? If there really is something like food in work and learning, then nothing is happier than a studious old age.[45] Scipio, we saw your father's friend Gallus in his labours, pretty much measuring the heavens and the earth. How often the day dawned on him when he'd be working on a chart begun at night – and how often night would creep up on him when he'd begun work in the morning! How happy he was to predict solar and lunar eclipses long before us!

50. Naevius rejoiced so much in his history of the Punic War, and Plautus in his plays *Truculentus* and *Pseudolus*. I also saw the elderly Livius Andronicus, who wrote a play during the consulships of Cento and Tuditanus, six years before I was born, and who was still alive right up to my own adolescence.

Why should I speak about Publius Licinius Crassus, with his study of religious and civil law, who was made high priest just a few days ago? Even so, we have seen all of those I've mentioned obsessed with their studies as old men. Yes, there was Marcus Cethegus, whom

Ennius rightly called 'the essence of persuasion' – I saw him work so hard on his rhetoric even when he was old. So where are the pleasures of feasting, gaming and whoring compared with these pleasures? These are the intense studies that accrue to the wise and well educated along with their years, so that it's an honourable thing that Solon said in a poem I mentioned before – that he grew old learning many things every day – and surely there can be nothing greater than the pleasure of the mind.

51. Now I come to the pleasures of agriculture, in which I take an unbelievable delight, none of which is hampered by old age and which seem to me the most appropriate to the life of a wise person. These pleasures have an account with the land, which never sends back a cheque and never returns what it takes without investing it, sometimes with less interest and more often with more. Still, it's really not just the fruit that delights me, but also the power and nature of the earth. In its soft, cultivated breast it draws in the sprinkled seed, hidden at first, which is why we call the process 'embedding';[46] then it spreads the seed, warmed by its humid embrace, and elicits green shoots from it; supported by the fibres of roots, it gradually reaches youth, and when erect, with knotty straw, as if reaching puberty, it is enfolded in a sheath; and when it emerges from that it pours its lined-up fruit with ranked points and is protected against the bite of smaller birds by a rampart of bristles.[47]

52. Why should I recollect the raising, sowing and growing of vines? I can never have enough of its delight, which you know is the joy and peace of my old age. And I omit the sheer strength of all the things that the earth

produces – the strength that can generate such great trunks and branches from something so tiny as a fig seed, or a grape pip, or from the most miniscule seeds of other fruits or shoots. Vine cuttings, tree cuttings or twigs, or new plants from split roots or shoots – don't they reliably delight anyone with the ability to admire them? Even the vine, which is floppy by nature, and ends up on the ground if it's not supported, will still raise itself by its tendrils as if somehow lifted by hands – it is a serpent that the farmer's art puts under control with swooping, wandering metal in case it becomes a forest of twigs and is poured out everywhere in its excess.

53. And so when approaching spring reaches those that are left, something called a bud – a jewel – arises on the limbs of the twigs, from which the growing grape reveals itself, and which, increasing with the moisture of the earth and the warmth of the sun, is bitter to the taste at first, before it sweetens on maturing, and, dressed in its foliage, it maintains just the right temperature and fends off the excessive rays of the sun. What could be more happily fruitful or visually beautiful than that? It's not just the vine's usefulness that delights me (as I've mentioned before); it's also the growing of the vine, and its very nature – the rows of supports, joining up the heads, tying vines down and propagating them, and that business I mentioned, of lopping some off and letting others go.

54. What should I say about irrigation, or about a field's ditches, or about frequent tilling, all of which make the earth much more productive? What should I say about the effectiveness of manuring? I said it in the book I wrote about country matters: the learned Hesiod said not

a word about it, even though he was writing about bringing up fields. But Homer, who seems to me to have written many centuries before him,[48] depicts Laertes softening the longing that he felt because of his son[49] by harvesting a field and putting dung on it. In fact, the joys of country life are not only in the crops, meadows, vineyards and woodlands, but also in gardens, orchards and more, in swarms of bees, in the variety of the world's flowers; and not only in planting but also in grafting, which is the cleverest thing agriculture has devised.

55. I could carry on about the many delights of rural affairs, but I feel that the things I have said are extensive enough. Still, you should forgive it: you see, I'm driven to distraction by my enthusiasm for farming, and old age is naturally loquacious (I shouldn't look like I'm exonerating it totally). It's why Marcus Curius lived out the last part of his life in this way, once he had conquered the Samnites, the Sabines and Pyrrhus. When I look at his house (it isn't far away from mine) I can't be more impressed than I am by the restraint of the man, or by the rigour of his times.

56. When the Samnites brought a great weight of gold to Curius, who was sitting at his fireplace, they were rebuked: he said, 'Having gold doesn't seem to be a distinction, but ruling those who have it does.' So was a such a great spirit somehow not able to make his old age pleasant?

But I'm coming back to farmers – I don't want to lose my thread. The senators – that is, the senior citizens – were in the fields when it was announced to Lucius Quintus Cincinnatus that he had been made dictator, and it was by his order that the master of the horse,

Caius Servilius Ahala, seized Spurius Maelius for seeking kingly powers and killed him.[50] Curius was summoned from his villa back to the senate, along with other old men, and for that reason the people who summoned him were called 'the travellers'.

So how can the old age of these people have been pitiable when they rejoiced in tilling the fields? In my opinion, I doubt if anything could be more blessed, not only through duty – because the cultivation of fields is healthy for the whole human species – but also, as I have said, through delight, and through the sufficiency and abundance of everything that is relevant to feeding people, and even to honouring the gods, so that we can now make our peace with pleasure, since some people crave these things. Yes, the cellar of a good and diligent master is full of wine, oil and also essentials, and the whole house is opulent as it abounds with pork, lamb, goats' meat, chicken, with milk, cheese and honey.[51] The same farmers call the garden a second butcher's. Falconry and hunting enhance life by their leisurely labours.

57. And what will I say about the greenness of meadows or rows of trees, or the diversity of vines and olives? I will be brief. Nothing can be more practically fruitful or aesthetically beautiful than a well-tilled field, and old age is no obstacle to this pleasure – moreover, old age actually welcomes and attracts it. After all, where else can someone of that vintage become warm by sunshine or by fire, or, alternatively, be cooled healthily by shade and water?[52]

58. So let others have their weapons, their horses, their spears, their training swords and their ball, their swimming[53] and

their racing – from their many sports they can leave us old folk dice and knuckle bones.[54] Take even that if you want, because old age is blessed without it.

59. Xenophon's books, which I beg you to go on reading eagerly, are devoted to many practical matters. He praises agriculture profusely in the book about household management (called *Economicus*). And so that you understand that nothing seemed as royal to him as the study of agriculture, in that book Socrates[55] talks with Critobolus about Cyrus the Younger, king of the Persians, outstanding in his wit and in the glory of his rule: when Lysander the Spartan (a man of utmost virtue) came to him at Sardis and brought him gifts from the allies, Cyrus was hospitable to Lysander in other ways, and showed him a carefully arranged park. When Lysander admired the extent of the trees, and the straight lines forming a quincunx, and the refined, pure soil, and the sweetness of the smells that wafted from the flowers, he said that he admired not only the care but also the skill of the man by whom all this was planned and designed. To which Cyrus replied, 'But I am the planner of all that; they are my rows, my design; many of those trees were sown by my hand.' Then Lysander, eyeing Cyrus' purple, the gleam of his body and his Persian costume bedecked with much gold and many gems, said, 'The people who say you're blessed are really right, Cyrus, because your good fortune is linked to virtue!'[56]

60. So old men can enjoy this good fortune, and old age doesn't prevent us from maintaining a passion for other things, but especially for agriculture, right up to the

end of our time. We're told that Marcus Valerius Corvinus lived on until his hundredth year, and when a normal lifespan would have been done, he was still living in his fields and cultivating them; forty-six years passed between his first consulship and the sixth.[57] So our ancestors wanted the time of our public careers to be a particular span in our ageing process; and its last phase is more of a blessing than the middle phase because there is more authority and less work.

Authority is the pinnacle of old age. How great was the authority of Lucius Caecilius Metellus, and Aulus Atilius Calatinus! This epitaph is about him:

Most people think this individual
was the pre-eminent man among the people.

That well-known poem is carved on his tomb. His authority was surely significant if the talk of him was about everyone's praise. What a man I saw in Publius Crassus, the high priest, and in his successor Marcus Lepidus, so distinguished in that religious role. And what about Paulus, and Africanus, or Maximus, whom I mentioned before? Their authority rests not only in an opinion from them, but even in a nod. Old age, and especially old age with honours, has the kind of authority that is greater than any youthful pleasure.

62. Bear in mind, though, that throughout this whole speech I am praising an old age that has been built on foundations laid in youth. From this follows something I once said with universal agreement: old age is wretched if it pleads for itself with a speech. No white hairs and no wrinkles can suddenly snatch away authority; but

an honourably spent prime of life wins the fruit of authority at life's end.

63. Those very things that seem trivial and common are actually honourable: that people pay you a morning visit, they seek you, they yield to you, they rise for you, they escort you from home, they escort you back home, they consult you – and among us, as in other societies, people are thought to be the most moral where these honours are most scrupulously observed. They say that Lysander the Spartan (whom I just mentioned) used to remark that Sparta was the noblest residence for the elderly because nowhere else is so much credited to old age; nowhere else is old age given more honours. For example, it's on record that when a mature man arrived in the theatre during the Athenian festival, none of his own fellow citizens in the large crowd gave up their place for him, but when he came to the Spartan seats (they had set seating because they were diplomats), it's said that they all rose for him and set aside a seat for the old man.

64. Upon this, when there was repeated applause from the whole crowd, one of the Spartans said that Athenians know what's right, but they don't want to do it.

There are many wonderful things about our College of Augurs, but this one is of foremost importance to our discussion: each member has precedence according to age and so takes the lead in debate, not only over those who outrank him; the elder augurs have precedence even over those who have official command.[58] So what are physical pleasures when compared with the rewards of authority? Those who have used this privilege seem to me to have finished the play of life splendidly, unlike the untrained mummers who collapse exhausted in the last act.

65. Oh, but the elderly are so morose and anxious and cranky and stubborn. It turns out they're misers too. But these are moral faults, not the faults of old age. But moroseness and the other faults I named do have a bit of an excuse – not a justification, but we can at least sympathise: old men think that they are ignored, hated and laughed at; what's more, every hurt is horrible for a frail body. But good habits and skills can make everything more pleasant, as we can see in life, and also in the brothers in the play *Adelphi*.[59] One of them is as irascible as the other is friendly! And so it goes: it's not every wine that turns to acid as it matures, and not every temperament either. I commend seriousness in old age, but, like everything, it should be moderate and not at all acerbic. And what avarice in the elderly can achieve, I really don't understand.

66. Is there anything more absurd than the traveller who looks for more luggage when there's little of the journey left?

There's the fourth charge left, which is the one that most acutely seems to make our time of life most troubled: the approach of death, which obviously can't be far away from old age. What sad old people they are who, their whole life long, will not have seen that death deserves their contempt! Clearly death is worth ignoring if it completely extinguishes our soul, or even worth choosing if it leads the soul to a place where it might live for ever. In any case, there can't be a third option available.

145

67. So what should I fear, if I'm not going to be sad or even happy after death? Can there be anyone, even a youth, who is so stupid as to anticipate that he might be alive this evening? If anything, that stage of life has more causes of death than mine: young people slip easily into illness, they suffer more severely, and the cures are more unpleasant.[60] As a result, few reach old age, and if that weren't the case, then life would be lived better, and more prudently. This is because intelligence, reason and forethought are properties of the elderly, and if there weren't any old people, then there would be absolutely no societies.

But I return to the subject of impending death. What horror does old age not share with youth?

68. Death is common to every age, as I have felt with my finest son, and as you have, Scipio, in your brothers, who were poised for most prestigious honour. Suppose the youth hopes that he will live for a long time, while the elderly can't hope for the same thing.[61] He hopes foolishly – after all, what could be more stupid than to mistake uncertainty for certainty, or the false for the true? Suppose the old man can't hope for anything. So? He's better in that state than the youth is, because what the youth hoped for has already happened to the old man: one wants to live for a long time, and the other has.

69. Still, good gods – what is there in human nature that does last for a long time? Suppose there's an extreme length of time: let's hope for the age of the southern Spanish king (I read[62] that Arganthonius of Cadiz ruled for 80 years and lived for 120) – even so, nothing seems to me to be a long time if there's an end to it, since

when the end comes, what has passed has ebbed away; the only thing left is what you have from your accomplishments, achieved properly and with virtue. The hours elapse, and days, and months, and years, and no time ever comes back, and no one can know what might follow. You should be happy with whatever time there is left for living.

70. You see, the performer doesn't have to act throughout the whole play to be entertaining – he'd win our approval if he were just in this or that act. And the elderly don't have to stay up until the sign comes up saying 'Applause',[63] because even our brief span of life is long enough for good and upright living; but if it goes on longer, it's no more painful than when farmers complain that spring's sweetness has passed and that summer and autumn have come. Spring, like youth, promises and shows the fruit of the future; the time that's left is suitable for eking out those fruits and appreciating them.

71. And, as I've often said, the fruit of old age is the remembering and amassing of fine accomplishments. Everything that comes about in accordance with the laws of nature should be taken as a blessing; and what could be more in accordance with nature than that the old should die?[64] When it happens to the young, their nature opposes it and fights back. So to me the young seem to die as the strength of a flame does when dowsed with water, whereas the elderly die when the consumed flame is extinguished without force and as if of its own accord; and just as apples are hard to pluck from the tree if they're unripe, but fall if they're mature and soft,

so force ends the young life, and maturity the old. The closer I come to death, it makes me happy that I seem to be sighting land, and about to reach the port after a long voyage.

72. But old age has no fixed end, and you live through it properly if you can pursue and maintain your duties, and if you can scorn death, so that old age can actually become livelier and stronger than youth. That's why Solon gave this answer to Pisistratus: when the tyrant asked what helped him to be so bold in his resistance, Solon replied, 'Old age.'[65] But the best end of life comes while the mind is intact, and the senses sure – when the same nature that put this work together now dissolves it. Just as the wright who built a ship destroys it easily, so it is best that nature dissolves the man whom it stuck together. Everything that's recently stuck together is taken down with difficulty, and the old easily.

And so it is that the elderly don't need to pursue greedily what's left of life, and it's not without reason that they should leave it.

73. Pythagoras forbids us to leave our sentry post until we're ordered by our commander – that is to say, God. There's a fragment of Solon the wise in which he says that he doesn't want his death to pass without the grief and mourning of his friends. I think he wants to seem dear to them. But I wonder if Ennius puts it better:

> No weeping honours me, nor is a tear
> part of my rites.

He doesn't think that death should be mourned when immortality is to follow.

74. Yes, there can be some sensation of the dying process, but it's a negligible time, especially for the old;[66] and after death, either there's a desirable feeling or there's nothing. But we need to think about this from our youth onwards, so that we can stop worrying about death; no one can live with a peaceful mind without this thought. It's certain that we must die, and not certain if it's to be today. So who can go about with a calm soul if he's fearing a death that's hanging over him every hour?

75. There doesn't seem to be any need to dispute this, since I don't remember Lucius Brutus disputing it when he was killed when liberating his country, nor the two Decii, who spurred their horses down the path to a willing death, nor Marcus Atilius, who set off for torture so that he could keep a promise to the enemy, nor the two Scipios, who wanted to block the Carthaginian advance with their own bodies, nor your grandfather Lucius Paulus, who, in the ignominy of Cannae, atoned by his death for the rashness of his colleague, nor Marcus Marcellus, whose burial not even his cruellest enemy allowed to take place without the honour of a funeral – rather, I remember our legions (as I've written in my *Histories*)[67] often setting out with a quick and upright spirit for positions from which they reckoned they could never return. Then why should learned old people fear something scorned by the young – not just the unlearned ones but also the crude?

76. Ultimately it seems to me a full enjoyment of all pursuits makes for a full enjoyment of life. Some pursuits are childish – do adolescents miss them? There are the pursuits of early adolescence – surely what we call middle age isn't fixed on them? As for the pursuits of that age – in

149

old age they're not required. There are those last pursuits of old age too. So, as the earlier pursuits pass, so do those of old age, and when that happens, there has been the full enjoyment of life, and the season for death has arrived.

77. So I don't see why I shouldn't tell you what I feel about death, because I seem to discern it better the closer I come to it. Scipio, Laelius, I consider that your fathers – those most distinguished men, and most dear to me – are still alive, and that this life is the only life worth recognising. It's because, while we're shut up in this structure of the body, we fulfil the obligations of fate and carry out hard labour; our heavenly soul is brought down from its highest home, as if it were sunk in the earth in a place quite opposite to eternity and divine nature.[68] But I believe that the gods scattered immortal souls in human bodies[69] so that there could be people who would protect the earth and whose contemplations of heavenly order might lead them to imitate it by the temperance and constancy of their lives. It's not just reason and debate that makes me believe this, but also the nobility and authority of our best philosophers.

78. I heard that Pythagoras and his disciples (who are nearly our compatriots, because they were once called the 'Italian philosophers') never doubted that our souls are outpourings from the divine universal mind. Besides that, there were proofs for me of what Socrates said on the last day of his life about the immortality of the soul – and the oracle of Apollo judged him to be the wisest of all men. Need I say more? I'm convinced of it, and I feel that because souls have such swiftness, such a memory of the past, such wisdom about the future, so many skills, so

many insights, so many inventions – because all these are so great, then whatever can contain that nature can't be mortal; and because the soul is always active without having a prime mover, because it moves itself, and will have no end of movement, because it never leaves itself; and because the nature of the soul is elemental and does not contain anything mixed in it that can be unequal or dissimilar to itself, then it can't be split, and if it can't be split it can't be undone; and people know many things before they are born, a great proof of which is that when children learn a difficult subject, they grasp innumerable things so quickly that they don't seem to be learning them for the first time, but to be remembering them and logging them. That's a summary of Plato.[70]

79. On his deathbed (according to Xenophon) Cyrus the Elder said this: 'My dear friends, when I am gone from you, do not consider that I will never exist, that I am nothing. While I was with you, you did not see my soul, but you knew it was in this body because of what I did. So you should believe it's still there, even if you don't see anything.

80. 'And really, no honour of distinguished men would linger if their souls did not bring it about that we would preserve their memory for longer. I could never be convinced that souls lived in mortal bodies but died when they left, nor that the soul is unconscious once it has left an unconscious body – rather that, when it is freed from all its bodily compound and begins to exist pure and intact, then it is fully conscious. And when a man's nature is dissolved by death, it's clear where each part departs, because everything goes back

to where it began; but only the soul is invisible, both when it's present and when it's gone. Really, there is nothing you see more like death than sleep.

81. 'Even so, the souls of sleepers proclaim their divinity the most, because when souls are remitted and free, they see much that is to come; which is how we can know what sort of futures those souls have once they've slipped completely from the chains of the body. And so if these things are true,' said Cyrus, 'you should cultivate me as if I were a god; but if the soul is buried with the body, then you will preserve my holy and untarnished memory respecting the gods who protect and govern the cosmos,' Cyrus said.

82. Cyrus saw this as he was dying. If it is pleasing, let us see it too. No one will convince me that your father Paulus, or your two grandfathers, Paulus and Africanus, or the father and uncle of Africans, or the many other distinguished men it is not necessary to list, applied themselves to those great things that stretched their memory to the future without perceiving in their souls that the future stretched out to them. Or, if I might boast about myself, a little in the manner of the elderly, do you think I would have undertaken such great tasks, either at home or on the battlefield, if the endpoint of my life would also be the limit of my fame? Wouldn't it have been better to live out a leisured and peaceful life without any toil and trouble? But somehow my soul arose and kept looking to the future, as if it would finally come alive once it had quit this life. And if it weren't the case that souls are immortal, then the souls of the best people wouldn't strive so fully for immortal glory.

83. What about the way the wisest of people die with their souls at peace, and the most stupid are restless? Surely the soul that sees more, and sees further, seems to regard itself as setting out for better things, whereas the soul with more obtuse acumen doesn't regard itself like that?

I am quite transported by the desire to see your fathers, whom I sought and whom I loved, and indeed I am eager to meet not only the people I've known, but also those about whom I've heard and read and even written; and once I've set out on my journey, it won't be at all easy to draw me back, even if you were to cook me up like Pelias.[71] And if any god were to arrange it for me that I could revert from this age to my childhood and could whimper in my cot, I'd vehemently refuse, as if I'd nearly finished the race only to be called back from the finishing line to the starting blocks.

84. After all, what comfort does life have? Or rather, what toil doesn't it have? Say it does have comfort – then surely that comfort will reach its fullness or its limit. I don't want to complain about life like many people do (including learned ones), and it doesn't irk me that I've lived, since I have lived in such a way that I reckon I wasn't born in vain, and I go from this life as if from a hotel and not from a house – because nature has given us a bed-and-breakfast rather than a home.

What a great day it will be when I set out for that divine council and congress of souls, and when I leave this rabble and jumble! You see, I'll be going not only to those about whom I spoke before, but also to my [son] Cato; no man born was better than he – no one more distinguished by his piety – whose body I cremated (the reverse, he burning me, would have been more fitting) and whose soul hasn't deserted me but keeps looking back – and who surely left for the place he knows is my own destination. When I looked as though I were bearing my situation bravely, it's not because I was taking it with a soul at peace, but because I was consoling myself that our parting, our separation, would not be long.

85. So, Scipio, Laelius, those are the factors behind what you are 'in the habit of admiring';★ why old age is light for me, and not only unencumbering but also happy. And if I'm wrong in my belief that human souls are immortal, then I'm glad to be wrong, and as long as I live I don't want this mistake, in which I rejoice, to be wrenched from me. But if I don't feel anything when I'm dead, as some small-time philosophers believe,[72] then I don't worry that those dead philosophers might be chuckling at my mistake. That's because, if we are not going to be immortal, then for a man to be extinguished when his time has come is a good option. Nature has a limit to life, as it has with everything else. The elderly phase of life is like the denouement of a play from which we should slip out when we're fatigued, and particularly when we've had enough.[73]

That's what I have to say about old age, which I pray that you reach, so that you can prove what you've heard from me by your own experience!

★ Cato is recalling Scipio's words at the start of this dialogue (4).

A final note on *On Old Age*

In our discussion of *On Old Age* so far I've drawn attention to its nostalgia and the writer's urge to preserve the past. It's true that Cicero, through Cato, honours his antecedents and, by implication, speaks up for a way of life that was already slipping away from him. But by the end we're allowed to think that Cicero has the future in mind, too. This is partly because he resolutely takes an optimistic view of death, to which subsequent readers have turned for consolation – Agnes Whitaker includes a substantial extract from Cicero's conclusion in *All in the End Is Harvest: An Anthology for Those Who Grieve;*[74] and it's also because he's looking at the futures of the young men to whom he's been talking all this while. One of them, P. Cornelius Scipio Africanus, became consul after Cato's death, and also a strict censor – Cato would have approved. He died in the violence that followed the land reforms proposed by Tiberius Gracchus: our Scipio was on the side that opposed the redistribution of land from the richer to the poorer classes. Laelius was a close friend of this Scipio, and took the same view of land reform. He, too, became consul.

In these respects, Cicero is looking forward (even though the whole dialogue is fixed deeply in the past). He's showing how good a future can be if you prepare for it – or at least if we listen to the elderly at just the right stage in our lives. But he's also reminding us that the elderly can look far into the future. When he broaches the subject of gardening, about which he later becomes almost comically passionate, he quotes Statius, who writes of an old man, 'He plants the trees to serve another age.' He is like the idealistic characters of Chekhov, such as Doctor Astrov in *Uncle Vanya*, who entertain a small hope that, if a tree they plant should last a thousand years, they will have done something to add to the happiness of much later generations.

Right from the start of the work, with its dedication, Cicero is clear that he wants his thoughts on old age to be useful: 'I want to free both you and myself from this burden, which we both share, of old age . . . philosophy can never be given enough of its due praise, since whoever is observant of it can live out any stage of his life untroubled.' How useful the work is depends on what use we in turn want to make of it, whether we're like Laelius and Scipio, listening to an authority on old age, or whether we're like the aged speaker. It's my hope that the work, and the context I offer for it, is at least, in Moses Finley's words, 'an aid to reflection' for those who are old or ageing and for those who may regard old age as a distant state of being, but still a state most of us aspire to reach.

Notes

Preface

1 Blake claimed that he was born in 1883.
2 Robert Garland, *The Greek Way of Life*, Duckworth, 1996, 248.
3 Quoted in Marie de Hennezel, *The Warmth of the Heart Prevents Your Body from Rusting*, Rodale, 2009, 44–5, translated by Susanna Lea Associates from *La chaleur du coeur empêche nos corps de rouiller*, Éditions Robert Laffont, 2008.
4 Socrates, *Laches*, 188c
5 Garland, 1996; Karen Cokayne, *Experiencing Old Age in Ancient Rome*, Routledge, 2003; Tim Parkin, *Old Age in the Roman World*, Johns Hopkins University Press, 2003.
6 I offer some reasons for this in the brief introduction to the text at page 105.

The Ancient Art of Growing Old

Introduction

1 The minister spoke on 18 October 2013 to the National Children and Adults Services conference: https://www.gov.uk/government/speeches/the-forgotten-million.
2 See discussion on www.mosqueonline.com

3 The report in the *Daily Mail* does more than others to emphasise the lower end of the scale: the 105 applies to girls on an estate in Northumberland, the 67 to boys in Birkenhead.

4 Parkin, 2003, 218.

5 Ibid, 226.

1. Looking back: How to make the most of the past

1 Jared Diamond, *The World Until Yesterday: What Can We Learn from Traditional Societies?*, Allen Lane, 2012, 216.

2 Moses Finley, 'The Elderly in Classical Antiquity', *Greece and Rome*, 28, 1981, 156–71; reprinted in Thomas M. Falkner and Judith de Luce, *Old Age in Greek and Latin Literature*, State University of New York Press, 1989, 58.

3 Section 56 is a possible exception, although the image of a well-stocked farmhouse proves Cato's point – it's *really* well stocked.

4 For example by Aviva: http://www.aviva.co.uk/pensions-and-retirement/retirement-centre/blog/roger-marsden/can-you-pass-the-marshmallow-test/. An excellent piece on the experiments limitations and procedural flaws comes from Carol Tauris in *The Times Literary Supplement*, 18 July 2014.

5 Plutarch, *Should the Elderly Run the Country?* 784b.

6 *Psychiatry*, 1963 26.63–76. The paper is discussed by de Luce, with reference to Ovid's late work, in Falkner and de Luce, 1989, 197ff. See also Butler's obituary in the *New York Times*: http://www.nytimes.com/2010/07/07/health/research/07butler.html?_r=0

7 Plutarch, *Should the Elderly Run the Country?* (*An seni respublica gerenda sit*) 784a; the Latin title is the most widely accepted one; my title's my own translation.

8 *New York Times*: http://www.nytimes.com/2010/07/07/health/research/07butler.html?_r=0

9 *Laws*, 4.721. Plato offers a related idea in his *Symposium*, but there he ranks the achievement of getting and rearing children as lower than writing, which in turn is lower than making laws.

2. What was old age?

1 This estimate comes from Parkin, 2003, who uses the Coale-Demeny Model Life Tables, based on later societies thought to be comparable, and from which more data is available.

2 From Robert Garland's entry 'Age', *Oxford Companion to Classical Civilization*, where he cites Keith Hopkins, *Population Studies*, 1966, 246–64.

3 Cokayne, 2003.

4 Given the difficulties of establishing this across a whole population, demographers use models of population and life-expectancy based on comparable societies that have yielded us more information. The model used by Tim Parkin is the Coale-Demeny West (Parkin, 2003, 280–1).

5 Bessie Richardson, *Old Age among the Ancient Greeks*, Johns Hopkins University Press, 1933, 231–6, with sources.

6 Parkin, 2003, 31.

7 Finley, 1981, 3; J. Eisinger, 'Lead and Wine', *Medical History*, 26, 1982, 279–302.

8 *BBC News Magazine*, 7 January 2013.

9 Parkin, 2003, 72.

10 Ibid. 251.

11 Horace, *Ars Poetica*, 158–78.

12 Horace, *Rhetoric*, II.12

13 Marie de Hennezel, *The Warmth of the Heart Prevents Your Body From Rusting*, Rodale, 2009, tr. Susanna Lea Associates.

14 de Hennezel, 78, quoting from a report by the French National Gerontology Foundation, *C'était hier et c'est demain: lettres d'anciens jeunes à de futurs vieux*, Taillander, Paris, March 2005.

15 We should bear in mind the debate we mentioned earlier, about how accurately scholars can estimate the age of death in ancient remains. But Joan P. Alcock lists a range of identifiable diseases, such as spinal tuberculosis, from a range of sites in *A Brief History of Roman Britain*, Robinson, 2011.

16 This was Galen's opinion too: he 'observed that the old were cold to the touch; he thought this was because they had lost nearly all the blood in their bodies' (*Mixtures*, 2.582). Cokayne, 2003, 37

17 Juvenal, *Satires*, 10, 217–19, 227–32.

18 Celsus, quoted by Cokayne, 2003, 37.

19 Karen Cokayne's highly efficient explanation has been invaluable to this discussion. Seneca treats old age as something that leads us towards death, and therefore the one death we can't avoid, *Epistulae morales*, 30.4: see Chapter 4, note 11 on *On Old Age* below).

20 Aristotle, *On Youth and Old Age, On Life and Death, On Breathing*, 4.

21 Ibid. 23.

22 Galen, *De Sanitate Tuenda* (On Hygiene), 5.9, quoted in Cokayne, 2003, 36.

23 'Motion and Rest: Galen on Exercise and Health', *Lancet*, Vol. 380. 9838, 21 July 2012, 210–11.

24 Cicero, *On Old Age*, sections 27 and 33.

25 We don't know the rules of this game, although the name suggests a focus on manual tackling, and from its context, at least in Galen, we can infer less aggression than we see in such non-natural games as rugby or American football.

26 de Hennezel, 16.

27 Mary Beard, *A Point of View*, BBC Radio 4, 9 May 2014.

28 http://www.bupa.co.uk/individuals/health-information/directory/e/exercise-older-people

3. Looking old

1 Interview in *Reader's Digest*, quoted in the *Daily Telegraph*, 18 September 2012.

2 de Hennezel, 62.

3 Juvenal, *Satires*, 10, 196–200.

4 Musei Vaticani, Museo Gregoriano Profano, ex-Lateranese, Rome

5 An image and a discussion of it are available on the Met's website: http://metmuseum.org/collections/search-the-collections/ 248132.

6 For example, Ovid, *Amores*, 1.8.

7 Horace, *Odes*, 1.25 seems all the nastier for lacking even this motivation.

8 Ovid, *The Art of Love*, 3.65–6, 69–76.

9 Romans imported human hair for this purpose: blonde hair came from Germany, and black hair from India. The same is true today, at least in Zadie Smith's *White Teeth*, in which Asian girls sell their hair so that Afro-Caribbean girls can extend theirs.

10 Ovid, *The Art of Love*, 3.159–68.

11 Synesius wrote *In Praise of Baldness* in about 402, in response to Dio Chrysostom's *In Praise of Hair*. I'm indebted to Tom Holland's tweet.

12 Richardson, 1933, 9, citing Aristotle, *Historia Animalium* 3. 518a, 26–8.

13 Martial, *Epigrams*, 3.43.

14 November, 262–71, with Nick Knight's accompanying portraits.

15 Phillips and one other of the eight participants in the discussion declined to say how old they were.

16 *The Times* (T2), 2 June 2014.

4. Old loving

1 E. Diehl (ed.), *Anthologia Lyrica Graeca*, 3rd edn, vol. 1, no. 1

2 Cicero, *On Old Age*, section 40.

3 See Cicero, *On Old Age*, section 51, and for a modern comparison, the *Onion*, 'My Seed Is Pure' http://www.theonion.com

4 Cicero, *De Officiis* (On Duties), 1.17.54.

5 Geoffrey Chaucer, *The Wife of Bath's Prologue*, 471–8.

6 Ovid is just as capable of writing of a woman's fading looks, in the context of saying, 'Gather ye rosebuds while ye may,' as he does at the start of *The Art of Love*, 3.

7   Ovid, *The Art of Love*, 2.663–8, 675–80, 693–700.

8   Ibid, 3.573–4.

9   Parkin, 2003, 87.

10 See Lysias, *Against Eratosthenes.*

11 Parkin, 2003, 198.

12 Nancy Demand, *Birth, Death, and Motherhood in Classical Greece*, Johns Hopkins University Press, 1994, 26.

13 Thucydides, *History of the Peloponnesian War*, 2.45.2.

14 *The Times Magazine*, 21 July 2012.

15 The *Daily Mail* story on Jacqueline Bisset was taken from an interview in the *Guardian* (24 July 2014), in which the interviewer, Catherine Shoard, showed no amazement that the actor was sexually active. The *Mail* ran two stories within a week about Susan Sarandon and her boyfriend. He was 36 in their report on 25 July 2014 and 37 on 27 July, which narrows down when his birthday is.

16 Emma Jane Kirby's report on BBC's *PM* programme (13 February 2014) explored this grey area.

5. The old in the home and the community

1   Homer, *Iliad*, 477–9.

2   Plato, *Laws*, 931–2, translated by Trevor J. Saunders, Penguin, 1970.

3   On the fifth age of men, see Hesiod, *Works and Days*, 170–85.

4   Euripides, *Alcestis*, 653–72.

5   And Parkin wrote his book before the 2008 crash, after which the younger generation had even less taxable income. See Parkin, 2003, 205. He cites, among other sources, M. S. Rendall and R. A. Bahchieva, 'An old-age security motive for fertility in the United States?', *Population and Development Review*, 24, 1998, 293–308.

6   Aristophanes, *Clouds*, 1413–19.

7   Parkin, 2003, 217–18, tells the extraordinary story, which he assures us is not historical, of a woman who was imprisoned and denied food, whose daughter breastfed her. When this was

discovered, the mother was freed and a temple built on the site of the prison (Pliny the Elder, *Natural History*, 7.36.121).

8 Horace, *Satires*, 2.5, 70–2.

9 Cicero, *On Old Age*, sections 65 and 66.

10 Garland, 1996, 257.

11 Richardson, 1933, 58.

12 See his scholarly and ground-breaking article '*Servi Senes:* the Role of Old Slaves at Rome' in *POLIS, Revista de ideas y formas políticas de la Antigüedad Clásica*, 8, 1996, 275–93.

13 Aristotle, *Rhetoric*, 2.13.

14 Euripides, *The Madness of Heracles*, 637–647.

15 Sophocles, *Oedipus at Colonus*, 3–6.

16 However, for a discussion of how dramatists presented Athens as an unusually accommodating city to supplicants, see D. M. Carter, *The Politics of Greek Tragedy*, Bristol Phoenix Press, 2007, 43.

17 Mark 12.41–4; Ovid, *Metamorphoses*, 8.611–724.

18 9 May 2014.

19 de Hennezel, 2009, 36.

6. The old in public life

1 This story, from the *Historia Augusta*, is quoted and discussed by Parkin, 2003, 106–7.

2 Garland, 1996, 284.

3 Cicero, *On Old Age*, sections 63–4.

4 Ovid, *Fasti*, 5.57–78.

5 Horace too refers to this custom (*Satires*, 2.5.16) and as we see in Cicero (for example at section 47, which is exceptional in the details, and more straightforwardly at section 63), it was befitting for an old man to have some sort of entourage.

6 The ancients, including Cicero, are keen to link the word 'senate' to *senex* ('old man'), but Parkin argues that *seniores* (elders) is truer to practice.

7 Parkin, 2003, 130–1.

8 Seneca, *Epistulae morales*, 36.

9 *Laws*, 2.666a–c.

10 *Today*, BBC Radio 4, 15 July 2014.

11 Atwood has since tweeted, 'I was not the first to nail the brain surgeon quip – it's been around – but it's always useful . . .'

7. The old mind

1 Juvenal, *Satires*, 10, 232–6.

2 *The Works of Jonathan Swift, D.D.*, ed. Walter Scott, Vol. 14, 329.

3 Cicero, *On Old Age,* section 21.

4 N. C. Berchtold and C. W. Cotman, 'Evolution in the Conceptualization of Dementia and Alzheimer's Disease: Greco-Roman Period to the 1960s', *Neurobiology of Ageing*, vol. 19, no. 3, 1998, 173–89

5 Cicero, *On Old Age*, section 36

6 See Thomas K. Hubbard's discussion of this (and of old men in the plays of Aristophanes) in Falkner and de Luce, 1989, 90–113. Connas was a flute player; the Prytaneion was where winning athletes could eat for free throughout their lives.

7 In Euripides, *Alcestis*, 653–72

8 'We're the Only Ones with Rights over Our Lives', *London Evening Standard*, 14 July 2014.

9 Lucretius, *On the Nature of Things*, 3.79–82.

10 Socrates' death can be seen as a kind of suicide, since he rejected the option of escaping from prison before his execution.

11 Seneca, *Epistulae morales*, 58.22.

12 *Epistulae morales*, 78.

13 *Epistulae morales*, 58.

14 *Epistulae morales*, 58.32–7.

15 This seems to have been such a serious condition that when Seneca was found guilty of sleeping with the emperor Caligula's daughter, he wasn't executed because he looked

likely to die anyway. He was exiled to Corsica instead, which could easily have done him more good than harm.

16 *Epistulae morales*, 78.14.

17 *Epistulae morales*, 78.10.

18 Seneca, Letter 12.

19 The Latin here translates as, 'He looks at the doors.' In the ancient world corpses in a house were laid down with their feet pointing to the door, as if about to leave.

20 A joke assuming that we agree with Pythagoras (and Shakespeare) that old age is a second childhood, and that we end up with as many teeth as we had when we were born.

21 *Skoteinos* means 'the obscure one'.

22 As Walter C. Summers explains in his selection of Seneca's letters, '*Parentalia* were festivals held during that part of the year which was specially devoted to the memory of the dead (February 13–21), and also on the anniversaries of the days on which the deceased was born or died.'

23 Horace takes up this theme (*Odes*, 3.29), and his lines endure to us through Dryden's translation (which are adapted in a song by the Northern Irish pop band the Divine Comedy): 'Happy the man, and happy he alone,/He, who can call to-day his own:/He who, secure within, can say/To-morrow do thy worst, for I have lived to-day!'

24 Seamus Heaney texted the Latin, '*Noli timere*,' to his wife on his deathbed. These were his last words.

25 The Greek equivalent of *necessitas* is *anangke*, which often means 'fate' – what has to be. And since 'what has to be' is what a Stoic trains himself to accept, this seems to make Seneca's closing remarks to his correspondent all the more surprising.

Conclusions

1 *Carpe diem*.

2 Homer, *Odyssey*, 24.250; *Iliad*, 19.336.

On Old Age

Cato the Elder on Old Age

1 Although Cicero often berates the thinking of Epicurus, he sometimes finds the language of Epicureanism helpful, and his Latin for 'untroubled', *sine molestia*, would be a useful rendering of the Epicurean goal of *ataraxia*.

2 The story of Tithonus doesn't suit Cicero, not only because it's a myth but also because it's a myth about how grim it would be to grow constantly old without hope of the ageing process ever coming to an end. Tithonus was the lover of Aurora, goddess of the dawn, who asked that he could have the gift of eternal life and then wished she'd asked that he could have eternal youth instead.

3 See Euripides, *The Madness of Heracles*, 637.

4 This seems all the worse when we learn that Albinus was 50 when he died (Parkin, 2003, 21). Seneca picks up on this when he says that lacking pleasures is a pleasure of its own (p.85 above), and at an early moment in Plato's *Republic*, on which the opening of *On Old Age* is closely based, we hear the anecdote about Sophocles, who says that old age has freed him from a cruel despot (as at section 47).

5 Herodotus tells a version of this story in his histories (8.125).

6 Cato is talking about the consul and general Fabius Cunctator, who was his hero, role model and patron. *Cunctator* means 'delayer' – a reference to the great man's steeliness and patience when confronting the threat of Hannibal during the Second Punic War. He captured Tarentum twice – the second time from Hannibal, in 212 BC.

7 Cicero uses the word *adolescentulus*, the diminutive form of *adolescens*, suggesting very young. But Cicero elsewhere refers to himself as *adolescentulus* when 27, indicating that age categories are flexible and sometimes relative to experience.

8 This is a characteristically austere stance for Cato to take – he

defended the idea that lawyers shouldn't receive fees, and that there should be limits on gifts of property.

9 The College of Augurs, of which Cato was a member (and which he singles out for praise in his speech, because it allows its oldest members to speak first), existed to advise Rome about what the omens suggested should be done. Fabius' contribution to this debate was to take the emphasis away from prophecy and to use Rome's safety as a starting point, so that the augur's job became to make the interpretation of omens fit the best course of action.

10 Cato will later refer to his own experience of this loss (at section 84), and it is a powerful reminder of Cicero's feelings on losing his daughter Tullia.

11 Isocrates (436–338 BC), a distinguished teacher of rhetoric, starved himself to death when Philip of Macedon defeated the Athenians and Thebans at the battle of Chaeronea.

12 We can't be sure about this, but he certainly reached an extra-ordinary age. He was born in about 485 BC; various dates for his death would make him somewhere between 105 and 108.

13 As Cato speaks, they are the current consuls, which puts Ennius' death at 169 BC, and the dialogue at 150 BC, the year before Cato's death.

14 Given Cato's later claim that the voice of an aged orator begins to fail him (section 28), the speaker's pride in his stamina is all the more pronounced. The law itself has some relevance to the subject of old age: no man worth 100,000 sesterces or more could make a woman his *heres* (at once heir and executor). A law made by Solon meant that the ancient Athenians had the right to question the will of an old man if he were thought to be of unsound mind, as the story about Sophocles (section 47) reminds us.

15 On Appius Claudius, see also section 37.

16 In fact, Cato and this grandfather had been bitter rivals. Scipio Africanus had defeated Hannibal at the battle of Zama in 202 BC, but Cato disapproved of his failure to see this victory

through with the destruction of Carthage. He also strongly disliked Scipio Africanus' conduct in public life after that. Africanus was the father of Publius Cornelius Scipio, who adopted the present Scipio. When our Scipio became consul for the second time, in 146 BC, Carthage was indeed destroyed. '*Delenda est Carthago*' was Cato's catchphrase: see *Asterix and the Laurel Wreath*.

17 See Ovid, *Fasti*, 5.57–78, quoted above at page 70, along with Parkin's view that the word indicated men who were older rather than necessarily old.

18 The highest body in the Spartan state consisted of 30 men. Two of these were the Spartan kings, and the rest had to be 60 years old or more. It was called the *gerousia*, and the name comes from the same root as our words 'geriatric', 'gerontology'.

19 A common estimate of the number of Athenian citizens (not women, not slaves, not foreigners) is 20,000.

20 The reference to court hearings is a sort of money joke: you were fined if you didn't appear. Cicero returns to this accusation at section 65, and appears to be echoing the sentiments of Aristotle, as well as caricatures of old men in the plays of Aristophanes, who show up for payments and the free soup.

21 Caecilius had clearly touched a nerve. In *Clouds* Aristophanes presents the shocking spectacle of a son beating his father. It's delightful that Cicero presents a model of the young admiring the old, but the laws that obliged the young to nurse and support the old, along with the observations of such writers as Hesiod, Aeschylus, Euripides, Plato, Aristophanes and onwards, are constant reminders that this didn't always happen.

22 For a Stoic philosopher, this is the best way to be sure of leading a life according to the order of nature.

23 I've often thought this – that the ideas we have in our youth can be fertile and numerous enough to give us projects into our old age.

24 As we can see from the introduction, Cicero had to invent

this interest of Cato's in Greek literature, in order to convey his own learning and his own admiration for Greek philosophers. In life, Cato the Elder was as opposed to Greek civilisation and values as it was possible to be.

25 Cokayne quotes Quintilian (as part of her argument that a greater degree of conservatism was expected of the elderly): 'a full haughty, bold and florid style would be less becoming to an old man than a restrained, mild and precise style . . .' Cicero's word for 'gentle' is *composita*.

26 Quaestors had responsibilities for maintaining the financial health of the state. In Cato's time there were ten of them. See also *Asterix in Switzerland*.

27 This is the exact opposite of a conclusion Marie de Hennezel reaches in conversation with Olivier de Ladoucette, who says, 'Life expectancy is growing less quickly than the expectancy of a life without disabilities. So there is no need to panic.' Cf. section 74.

28 'Peak dryness' – *siccitas* is sometimes translated as 'wiriness' but Cicero's choice of word here is revealing, as if to suggest that the dryness that Galen came to see as a natural result of ageing from birth onwards is somehow an actual advantage to the old. At least, to Reid in his edition, it suggests a freedom from colds. He quotes Varro: 'Because of their moderate exercises, the Persians attained that dryness of the body, so that they didn't spit, or wipe their noses, and so their body is scarcely puffed out.' *De Senectute*, edited by James Reid, Cambridge, 1879.

29 This is a reference to the physical labour that was required of all Roman citizens – the *munera personalia* – contributions you would make in person. Each man could spend up to five days working on public projects such as roads, buildings or transport. See Parkin, 2003, 129ff.

30 Several writers recommended wine as a way of alleviating old age, and even Solon took more pleasure in wine towards the end of his life – see Richardson, 1933, 29. It's worth

noticing that Cicero doesn't ban wine, but here, as elsewhere, urges moderation.

31 It's likely that Cicero was thinking of Pappus, a stock character of the farces Romans enjoyed, who was recognisable by his infirmity and naivety.

32 Some massive ifs.

33 In the introduction to his edition of this dialogue (p22) Reid calls this 'the first real historical work in Latin. [Cato's] predecessors had been merely compilers of chronicles. The work was founded on laborious investigations, and comprised the history of Rome from the earliest times to 150 BC . . .' Some fragments of *Origines* survive.

34 'Couch' should be understood more as a (comfortable) office chair than a chaise longue or bed.

35 Somehow it's hard not to think of how Oscar Wilde embraces this aspect of pleasure, as he does in his discussion of smoking: 'A cigarette is the perfect type of a perfect pleasure. It is exquisite, and it leaves one unsatisfied. What more can one want?'

36 For a good republican Roman (as Cicero had been) 'kingdom' means tyranny.

37 Archytas seems to miss the point that, for some, this is the very pleasure they seek.

38 This spate of name-dropping seems meant to impress us at once with Cato's mental agility and Cicero's scholarship. Plato would have been 79 at the time, 'and too old, it is thought, to have visited Italy,' writes W. A. Falconer in his translation (Loeb Classical Library, 1923). But then Plato has already served Cicero as an example of active old age.

39 Cicero here puts pleasure and virtue in direct opposition, and in so doing appears to be setting the distinct schools of Epicureanism and Stoicism against each other. But the accusation that Epicurus and his followers valued pleasure alone and for its own sake is more a caricature than a criticism. Although virtue for its own sake was indeed a Stoic goal and

not an Epicurean one, the forethought that Cicero imagines to be so lacking in his hedonistic Aunt Sally was exactly what Epicureans such as Lucretius wanted us to have: a short-term pleasure is not worth having if it leads to longer-term discomfort. But Cicero was aware that a useful Greek word for this kind of forethought, mental control and moderation is *sophrosune*, and that it was a vital word for the Epicurean writer Democritus. As we've heard the Stoic Seneca say above, '"Epicurus said that!" you say. "What are you doing with someone else's material?" If it's true, it's mine. I will keep Epicurus working on you, so that those people who swear by speakers rather than valuing what they say, might know that the best things are shared.'

40 As Reid explains, Decius 'gave his life as a propitiatory offering to the powers of the unseen world, in order to bring victory to the Roman arms'. He adds that Decius' father had done the same thing.

41 It's hard to find an equivalent word in English. The word *sodalis*, or 'fellowship', denotes an ancient society or club that existed to honour certain rituals. Reid offers 'brotherhoods' (ibid.).

42 'Early dinners' – *tempestiva convivia* – were dinners that started before the usual time, which was about 3 p.m. The phrase was a byword for decadent behaviour. It's a fittingly Roman touch, though, that decadence means starting your debauch early rather than indicating that it is to go on late.

43 See Seneca, *Epistulae morales,* 12.

44 *Bona aetas.* The fact that 'a good age' is a term for youth tells us something about the prevalence of the attitudes Cicero is challenging.

45 The Latin *otiosa* has the sense of leisure – its negative, *negotium*, means 'business' – and yet *otium* normally refers to the pleasure derived from literary pursuits, hence our word 'otiose', with its sense of an academic pursuit or enquiry that is all but pointless.

46 He means harrowing, but Cicero is talking about the aspect of harrowing that covers the seed.

47 The sexual nature of this passage is unmistakable in the Latin, which takes the theme of sublimating sexual energy further than even Ovid does. In his *Cures for Love* the poet offers farming as a substitute for love, and finds it hard to avoid language suggestive of fertility. Cicero's use of the technique seems less ironic: nature amply replicates the pleasures of which old age deprives us. They are more enduring, too, because the elderly who pursue them are thinking of future generations (see Statius, quoted in section 24); this is why Cicero has Cato stress that his love of farming is not only in the crop but also in nature itself.

48 Note that being an earlier writer is a natural criterion for being judged a better one.

49 Cato is talking about the scene at the end of the *Odyssey* in which Odysseus reveals to his father that he is alive (after a teasing delay). Laertes is farming, but Homer doesn't mention muck-spreading. See also Thomas M. Falkner's essay *Epi geraos oudo – Homeric Heroism, Old Age and the End of the Odyssey,* Falkner and de Luce, 1989, 21–67.

50 Cincinnatus is best known for being the old man who was working in a field when the senate asked him to return as dictator, to lead Rome against the Aequians and the Sabines. He was working the land and living in a cottage because he had withdrawn from public life following the disgrace of his son. Cato is here talking about Cincinnatus' second recall to the dictatorship. The summary execution of Spurius Maelius that Cato mentions was considered a heroic act at the time, but Maelius' crime seems not so bad: he was distributing corn in a time of famine, and was accused of trying to become king by winning the people's favour (as Reid's note explains). If this sounds reactionary, it's clearly not a perception that bothers Cato.

51 It may not be Cato's intention, or Cicero's, to sound rich,

especially since the speaker's constant refrain is the benefit of modesty and restraint. But this sounds like a more than well-stocked house. Virgil wrote his *Georgics* after Cicero wrote this essay, but he offers the figure of the shepherd from Corcyra (4.125–138) who triumphs over the obstacles that difficult land presents, to 'weigh his table down with unbought feasts'. Virgil mentions nothing of meat, and it's tempting to see this self-sufficiency and self-discipline as a more universal model for a Roman audience looking for ways to live out a comfortable old age. But Cicero's readers, along with Cato's audience (of distinguished young men), are more likely to have been privileged than the many illiterate citizens around them. Virgil praises the even simpler life.

52 The insertion of the word 'healthily' looks redundant at first, because it appears alongside the cooling part and not the warming part. I tentatively suggest that this is because Cicero is bearing in mind those ancient medical principles, expounded particularly by Aristotle, asserting that life is sustained by heat, and so Cicero needs to qualify his remarks by suggesting that there is a sort of cooling that is healthy.

53 Reid suggests that the Latin text can be sensibly emended to offer 'hunting' instead of 'swimming'. (He makes this reading sound possible but not obvious.)

54 Knuckle bones, as Reid explains, were oblong and had the numbers 1, 6, 3 and 4 on them (1 was opposite 6). He adds, 'These games, which were forbidden by many ineffectual laws … were held to be permissible for old men.'

55 As Plato did, so Xenophon too made Socrates a speaker in his dialogues. In Xenophon's work Socrates sounds less like a riddler and a questioner, and more like an authoritative Dr Johnson figure with memorable table talk.

56 This anecdote is a fairly close translation of Xenophon's *Economicus* (4.20–5). I think it can be seen as a useful link between the digression on farming and a line of thinking that characterises the whole essay: the idea that a virtuous

hard-working life is essential to a happy old age, but along with that the more implicit understanding that some people are more likely to have the resources necessary to a comfortable old age than others. It reminds us of Cato's earlier remarks about Ennius – that he lived out a meagre old age as if he'd been born for it. The message remains: if you're a fortunate person, you can still blow your retirement through a lack of virtue; and if you're unfortunate, you can still make the best of your situation. Best of all, though, is to be fortunate and virtuous – not unlike Cato himself, and a bit less like Cicero, whose world was collapsing around him.

57 A note from Reid corrects this: Corvinus was consul first in 348 BC, and last in 299 BC, so 49 years.

58 That is to say, if a speaker is older, he speaks before anyone even with the rank of knight, praetor, consul, governor or dictator.

59 By Terence (c.194–159 BC).

60 This is thought by some to be an observation taken from Hippocrates.

61 Cf. Seneca, *On the Shortness of Life*, 3: 'What, then, is the reason of this? You live as if you were destined to live for ever; no thought of your frailty ever enters your head, you take no heed of how much time has already gone by. You squander time as if you drew from a full and abundant supply, though all the while that day which you bestow on some person or thing is perhaps your last.'

62 Herodotus, *Histories* 1, 163.

63 As with studio audiences now, so with the Roman stage – the word 'applaud' was often written into Plautus' scripts, and always with Terence, which is another sign that Plautus was at least slightly funnier.

64 Another clear statement of the Stoic position.

65 The suggestion here is that Solon is so little afraid of death that he can behave in this reckless way. Plutarch slants this slightly differently in his '*Should the Elderly Run the Country?*'

The fuller context offers a different interpretation: in Plutarch, Solon leaves weapons outside his house for the young to use because it's old age that makes him resist Pisistratus in this way rather than in a more combative one. Aristotle covers the showdown in his *Athenian Constitution*: Solon refused to give up his own bodyguard to Pisistratus, saying that this made him wiser than half the people, who couldn't foresee the tyranny, and braver than the rest, who could see it but put up no resistance. When this made no difference, 'he carried out his armour and set it up in front of his house, saying that he had helped his country as far as he could (he was already a very old man), and that he called on all others to do the same. Solon's exhortations, however, proved fruitless.'

66　Cf. Seneca, *Epistulae morales*, 30.4: 'In old age alone, there is no interceding. There is no other way for people to die more gently, nor to be dying over a longer period.'

67　The *Origines*

68　This line of thought, and the respect of the soul alongside the denigration of the body, owes much to Plato, and in particular the *Phaedo*, in which Socrates contemplates his own death and afterlife. But, as Reid points out, there is an overlap with Cicero's own Stoic line of thought: 'the Stoics laid great stress on the ethical value of a contemplation and imitation of the order of the universe.'

69　There is a note here of the Orphic belief that our bodies contain a spark of the divine. The followers of Orpheus' cult thought that this was from dust left over from the remains of the Titans after they were defeated by the gods of Mount Olympus.

70　Plato develops this last idea, called *anamnesis*, in the *Phaedo*, and proposes it first in the *Meno*, in which Socrates guides a slave boy towards the right answer to a geometrical question, and proposes that this is because he always knew the answer but had forgotten it on being born. In this view of life's end, Cicero is attracted to the idea that, far from old age being a time of forgetting, it could perhaps be drawing ever closer to the time for knowing everything.

71 Cicero is thinking of the moment when Medea chops up Jason's father Aeson and boils him up in a cauldron. The result is that he re-emerges with his youth restored. This is how she successfully persuades Pelias' daughters to do the same to Pelias – and how she gets rid of him.

72 A direct dig at the Epicureans, who really did believe this.

73 This is the closest Cicero comes in this text to discussing suicide. As we've seen, Seneca is much franker about the subject, even if he adopts slightly different stances on it at different times.

74 Darton, Longman & Todd, 1984.

THE HISTORY OF VINTAGE

The famous American publisher Alfred A. Knopf (1892–1984) founded Vintage Books in the United States in 1954 as a paperback home for the authors published by his company. Vintage was launched in the United Kingdom in 1990 and works independently from the American imprint although both are part of the international publishing group, Random House.

Vintage in the United Kingdom was initially created to publish paperback editions of books bought by the prestigious literary hardback imprints in the Random House Group such as Jonathan Cape, Chatto & Windus, Hutchinson and later William Heinemann, Secker & Warburg and The Harvill Press. There are many Booker and Nobel Prize-winning authors on the Vintage list and the imprint publishes a huge variety of fiction and non-fiction. Over the years Vintage has expanded and the list now includes great authors of the past – who are published under the Vintage Classics imprint – as well as many of the most influential authors of the present. In 2012 Vintage Children's Classics was launched to include the much-loved authors of our youth.

For a full list of the books Vintage publishes,
please visit our website
www.vintage-books.co.uk

For book details and other information about the classic authors we publish, please visit the Vintage Classics website
www.vintage-classics.info

www.vintage-classics.info